Anne Hébert: Selected Poems

Anne Hébert:

Selected Poems

Translated by
A. Poulin, Jr.

BOA Editions, Ltd.
Brockport, N.Y.
1987

Grateful acknowledgment is made to the editors of publications in which earlier versions of these translations and of the Afterword originally appeared: *The American Poetry Review, F.A.R.O.G. Forum, Graham House Review, Ms., New England Review and Breadloaf Quarterly, The Noiseless Spider, Quarterly Review of Literature, Tar River Poetry, Voyages, A Book of Women Poets from Antiquity to Now* (Aliki Barnstone & Willis Barnstone, eds. New York: Schocken Books, 1980) and *The Contemporary World Poets* (Donald Junkins, ed. New York: Harcourt Brace Jovanovich, 1976).

‿

ISBN 0-918526-56-6 Cloth   LC # 87-71303
   0-918526-57-4 Paper

‿

Cover Design: Daphne Poulin

Cover Painting: "Katrin and Her Cat # 2" by Robert Marx; from the private collection of Mr. & Mrs. J. Godfrey Crowe.

Typesetting: Sans Serif, Inc., Ann Arbor, Michigan

BOA logo: Mirko

Published simultaneously in Canada by Stoddart Publishing, Co., Ltd., 34 Lesmill Road, Don Mills, Ontario, M3B 2T6.

BOA Editions, Ltd.   First Edition: December, 1987
92 Park Avenue
Brockport, NY 14420

‿

The publication and distribution of
Anne Hébert: Selected Poems
by BOA Editions, Ltd. was made possible
with the generous assistance of:

The Délégation du Québec;
The Arts Promotion Department of
The Department of External Affairs of Canada;
The New York State Council on the Arts; and
The National Endowment for the Arts.

Ève, Ève, nous t'appelons du fond de cette paix soudaine comme si nous nous tenions sans peine sur l'appui de notre coeur justifié.

Que ta mémoire se brise au soleil, et, au risque de réveiller le crime endormi, retrouve l'ombre de la grâce sur ta face comme un rayon noir.

— Anne Hébert

*These translations are for
my brothers and sisters*

—A. P., Jr.

CONTENTS

from **The Mystery of The Word**

Uncollected Poems

PREFATORY NOTE

As with many other collections of this kind, *Anne Hébert: Selected Poems* represents only one translator's selections and renderings of the poet's work into English.

Readers of this book who wish to become more familiar with the poetry of Anne Hébert in French and/or in English translation are encouraged to read the following other collections published to date:

FRENCH TEXTS:

Poèmes. Anne Hébert. Paris: Éditions du Seuil, 1960.

FRENCH AND ENGLISH TEXTS:

St-Denys Garneau & Anne Hébert. Translated by F. R. Scott. Vancouver: Klanak Press, 1962.
Dialogue sur la Traduction. Anne Hébert et Frank Scott. Montréal: Éditions HMH, 1970.

ENGLISH TEXTS:

The Tomb of Kings. Translated by Peter Miller. Toronto: Contact Press, 1967.
Poems by Anne Hébert. Translated by Alan Brown. Don Mills, Ontario: Musson Book Co., 1975.
Poems. Translated by A. Poulin, Jr. Princeton: Quarterly Review of Literature Poetry Series XXI: 3/4 1980.

I wish to thank the Research Foundation of the State University of New York for fellowships, the State University of New York, College at Brockport, for sabbaticals and The Embassy of Canada for a Faculty Enrichment Programme Grant—all of

14

which enabled me to complete these translations and to discuss them at length with Anne Hébert on more than one occasion.

Michel Gaulin introduced me to the work of Anne Hébert—ah, so many years ago—and read the manuscript of this book through its various stages, as did Peter Makuck. I am immeasurably grateful to each of them, not only for his expertise but also for his friendship.

I am also profoundly grateful to Anne Hébert for her patience, her many suggestions, her graciousness and for granting me permission to publish this selection of my translations of her wonderful poems.

—A. Poulin, Jr.
Brockport, N.Y.
March, 1987

Anne Hébert:
Selected Poems

Le Tombeau
Des Rois

The Tomb
of Kings

LES PÊCHEURS D'EAU

Les pêcheurs d'eau
Ont pris l'oiseau
Dans leurs filets mouillés.

Toute l'image renversée;
Il fait si calme
Sur cette eau.

L'arbre
En ses feuilles
Et dessin figé du vent
Sur les feuilles
Et couleurs d'été
Sur les branches.

Tout l'arbre droit,
Et l'oiseau,
Cette espèce de roi
Minuscule et naïf.

Et puis, aussi,
Cette femme qui coud
Au pied de l'arbre
Sous le coup de midi.

Cette femme assise
Refait, point à point,
L'humilité du monde,
Rien qu'avec la douce patience
De ses deux mains brûlées.

THE WATERY FISHERMEN

The watery fishermen
Have caught a bird
In their wet nets.

The whole scene capsized;
It's so calm
On this water.

The tree
In its leaves
The wind's shape frozen
In the leaves
And summer's colors
On the branches.

The whole tree straight,
And this bird,
A kind of king,
Tiny and naive.

And this woman,
Too, sewing
At the foot of the tree
Under the stroke of noon.

This sitting woman
Is mending, point by point,
The world's humility
With nothing but the tender patience
Of her two burnt hands.

LES MAINS

Elle est assise au bord des saisons
Et fait miroiter ses mains comme des rayons.

Elle est étrange
Et regarde ses mains que colorent les jours.

Les jours sur ses mains
L'occupent et la captivent.

Elle ne les referme jamais.
Et les tend toujours.

Les signes du monde
Sont gravés à même ses doigts.

Tant de chiffres profonds
L'accablent de bagues massives et travaillées.

D'elle pour nous
Nul lieu d'accueil et d'amour

Sans cette offrande impitoyable
Des mains de douleurs parées
Ouvertes au soleil.

HANDS

She sits on the edge of seasons
And flashes her hands like rays.

She is strange
And looks at her hands colored by days.

The days on her hands
Occupy and arrest her.

She never closes them
And she always stretches them.

The signs of the world
Are etched on her fingers.

So many deep markings
Weighing her down with massive wrought rings.

Between her and us
There is no place for rest and love

Without this ruthless offering
Of hands adorned with pain
Opened to the sun.

PETIT DÉSESPOIR

La rivière a repris les îles que j'aimais
Les clefs du silence sont perdues
La rose trémière n'a pas tant d'odeur qu'on croyait
L'eau autant de secrets qu'elle le chante

Mon coeur est rompu
L'instant ne le porte plus.

MINOR DESPAIR

The river's reclaimed the islands I loved
The keys of silence are lost
The hollyhock's not as sweet as I thought
The water has more secrets than it sings

My heart collapses
The moment no longer supports it.

NUIT

La nuit
Le silence de la nuit
M'entoure
Comme de grands courants sous-marins.

Je repose au fond de l'eau muette et glauque.
J'entends mon coeur
Qui s'illumine et s'éteint
Comme un phare.

Rythme sourd
Code secret
Je ne déchiffre aucun mystère.

A chaque éclat de lumière
Je ferme les yeux
Pour la continuité de la nuit
La perpétuité du silence
Où je sombre.

NIGHT

Night
The silence of the night
Engulfs me
Like vast underwater currents.

I rest at the bottom of mute and sea-green water.
I hear my heart
Flashing on and off
Like a lighthouse.

Pulsing rhythm
Secret code
I can't decipher any mystery.

With each flash of light
I close my eyes
To continue this night
Perpetuate this silence
Where I'm shipwrecked.

LES PETITES VILLES

Je te donnerai de petites villes
De toutes petites villes tristes.

Les petites villes dans nos mains
Sont plus austères que des jouets
Mais aussi faciles à manier.

Je joue avec les petites villes.
Je les renverse.
Pas un homme ne s'en échappe
Ni une fleur ni un enfant.

Les petites villes sont désertes
Et livrées dans nos mains.

J'écoute, l'oreille contre les portes
J'approche une à une toutes les portes,
De mon oreille.

Les maisons ressemblent à des coquillages muets
Qui ne gardent dans leurs spirales glacées
Aucune rumeur de vent
Aucune rumeur d'eau.

Les parcs et les jardins sont morts
Les jeux alignés
Ainsi que dans un musée.

Je ne sais pas où l'on a mis
Les corps figés des oiseaux.

SMALL TOWNS

I'll give you small towns.
Some very sad small towns.

The small towns in our hands
Are more austere than toys
But just as easy to handle.

I play with the small towns.
I topple them.
No man escapes
No flower nor child.

The small towns are deserted
And surrendered in our hands.

I listen, my ear against the doors.
I approach each and every door
With my ear.

The houses are like mute shells:
In their icy spirals
No murmur of wind
No whisper of water.

The parks and gardens are dead,
Games lined up
As in a museum.

I don't know where they've put
The stiff bodies of the birds.

Les rues sont sonores de silence.
L'écho du silence est lourd
Plus lourd
Qu'aucune parole de menace ou d'amour

Mais voici qu'à mon tour
J'abandonne les petites villes de mon enfance.
Je te les offre
Dans la plénitude
De leur solitude.

Comprends-tu bien le présent redoutable?
Je te donne d'étranges petites villes tristes,
Pour le songe.

The streets ring with silence.
The echo of silence is heavy
Even heavier
Than any word of love or threat.

But now it's my turn.
I abandon the small towns of my youth.
I offer them to you
In the fullness
Of their loneliness.

Do you really understand this dreadful gift?
I give you strange small towns
For dreams.

INVENTAIRE

Dans un réduit
Très clair et nu
On a ouvert son coeur
Et toute pitié:

Fruit crevé
Fraîche entaille
Lame vive et ciselée
Fin couteau pour suicidés.

Le sang (qui n'étonne personne)
Rutile
Goutte à goutte
(Quand il brunira
Nous serons loin
Et bien à couvert.)

Des deux mains plongées
Nous avons tout saisi
Tout sorti:

Livres chiffons cigarettes
Colliers de verre
Beau désordre
Lit défait
Et vous chevelure abandonnée.

Joies bannies
Désespoirs troués
Nul insolent trésor
En ostensoir

INVENTORY

In a hiding place
Bright and naked
We opened our heart
For pity's sake.

Burst fruit
Fresh slash
Sharp and chiseled blade
Good knife for suicides.

The blood (astonishing no one)
Gleams
(When it browns
We'll be far away
And well under cover.)

Plunging our two hands in
We grabbed everything
Dragged everything out:

Books rags cigarettes
Glass necklaces
Lovely disorder
Unmade bed
And you, abandoned hair.

Outlawed joys
Torn despairs
Not one insolent treasure
For a monstrance.

La châsse d'or
Que nous avions faite au mystère
Se dresse pillée
Spacieux désert.

Sur une table sans pieds
Son propre visage rongé
Qu'on a aussitôt jeté.

The golden shrine
We made for mystery
Stands plundered
Broad desert.

On a table without legs
Our own gnawed face—
We threw it right out.

VIEILLE IMAGE

Tout detruire
Le village
Et le château

Ce mirage de château
A la droite
De notre enfance.

L'allée de pins
Se ravine
Comme un mauvais chemin

Et nous marchons
Dans cet abîme
Se creusant.

Les pas des morts
Les pas des morts
Nous accompagnent
Doux muets.

Nous affichons
Notre profonde différence
En silence:

La rage
Qui oppresse notre poitrine
La corde que nous tenons
Et la poutre d'ébène
Que nous cherchons
Au grenier
De la plus douce tourelle.

OLD PICTURE

Destroy everything
The village
And the castle

This mirage of a castle
To the right
Of our childhood.

The lane of pines
Ruts itself
Like a bad road

And we walk
Into those chasms
Getting deeper.

Footsteps of the dead
Footsteps of the dead
Accompany us
Kind mutes.

We flaunt
Our utter difference
In silence:

The rage
Oppressing our chests
The rope we carry
And the ebony beam
We look for
In the attic
Of the sweetest turret.

Et, vieille image
Château village
Croulent au soleil
Sous le poids léger
D'un seul pendu.

And, old picture
Castle village
Crumble in the sun
Under the light weight
Of only one, hanged.

LA FILLE MAIGRE

Je suis une fille maigre
Et j'ai de beaux os.

J'ai pour eux des soins attentifs
Et d'étranges pitiés

Je les polis sans cesse
Comme de vieux métaux.

Les bijoux et les fleurs
Sont hors de saison.

Un jour je saisirai mon amant
Pour m'en faire un reliquaire d'argent.

Je me pendrai
A la place de son coeur absent.

Espace comblé,
Quel est soudain en toi cet hôte sans fièvre?

Tu marches
Tu remues;
Chacun de tes gestes
Pare d'effroi la mort enclose.

Je reçois ton tremblement
Comme un don.

THE THIN GIRL

I am a thin girl
And I have lovely bones.

I take care of them
And pity them strangely.

I polish them endlessly
Like old metals.

Jewels and flowers
Are out of season.

One day I'll seize my lover
To make myself a silver reliquary.

I'll hang myself
In his absent heart's place.

Who is this
Cold and unexpected guest in you, filled space?

You walk,
You stir,
Each of your gestures
A frightful ornament in a bezel of death.

I receive your trembling
Like a gift.

Et parfois
En ta poitrine, fixée,
J'entrouvre
Mes prunelles liquides

Et bougent
Comme une eau verte
Des songes bizarres et enfantins.

And sometimes,
In your breast, fixed,
I half open
My watery eyes:

Bizarre and childish dreams
Stir
Like green water.

LA CHAMBRE FERMÉE

Qui donc m'a conduite ici?
Il y a certainement quelqu'un
Qui a soufflé sur mes pas.
Quand est-ce que cela s'est fait?
Avec la complicité de quel ami tranquille?
Le consentement profond de quelle nuit longue?

Qui donc a dessiné la chambre?
Dans quel instant calme
A-t-on imaginé le plafond bas
La petite table verte et le couteau minuscule
Le lit de bois noir
Et toute la rose du feu
En ses jupes pourpres gonflées
Autour de son cœur possédé et gardé
Sous les flammes oranges et bleues?

Qui donc a pris la juste mesure
De la croix tremblante de mes bras étendus?
Les quatre points cardinaux
Originent au bout de mes doigts
Pourvu que je tourne sur moi-même
Quatre fois
Tant que durera le souvenir
Du jour et de la nuit.

Mon cœur sur la table posé,
Qui donc a mis le couvert avec soin,
Affilé le petit couteau
Sans aucun tourment
Ni précipitation?
Ma chair s'étonne et s'épuise

THE CLOSED ROOM

Who led me here?
Surely someone
Breathed on my heels.
When did that happen?
With what quiet friend's complicity?
The total consent of what long night?

Who designed this room?
In what calm moment
Did someone dream up the low ceiling
The small green table and tiny knife
The bed of black wood
And that whole rose of fire
In its swollen purple skirts
Around her heart possessed and guarded
By the orange and blue flames?

Who took the precise measurements
Of my extended arms' trembling cross?
The four cardinal points
Originate at my fingertips
Provided I turn on myself
Four times
As long as the memory
Of day and night will last.

My heart poised on the table,
Who set the silverware so carefully,
Sharpened the tiny knife
Painlessly
And without hurry?
My flesh is astonished and exhausted

Sans cet hôte coutumier
Entre ses côtes déraciné.
La couleur claire du sang
Scelle la voûte creuse
Et mes mains croisées
Sur cet espace dévasté
Se glacent et s'enchantent de vide.

O doux corps qui dort
Le lit de bois noir te contient
Et t'enferme strictement pourvu que tu ne bouges.
Surtout n'ouvre pas les yeux!
Songe un peu
Si tu allais voir
La table servie et le couvert qui brille!

Laisse, laisse le feu teindre
La chambre de reflets
Et mûrir et ton cœur et ta chair;
Tristes époux tranchés et perdus.

Without its customary guest
Between its rooted ribs.
The clear color of blood
Seals that deep vault
And my crossed hands
On this devastated place
Freeze, enchanted by space.

Oh soft sleeping body
The ebony bed contains you
And fits perfectly as long as you don't stir.
Especially don't open your eyes!
Dream a little
As if you saw
Such a table setting and the shining silver!

Oh let the fire dye
The room with gleams
And let your heart and flesh ripen:
Sad mates sliced and lost.

LA CHAMBRE DE BOIS

Miel du temps
Sur les murs luisants
Plafond d'or
Fleurs des noeuds
        cœurs fantasques du bois

Chambre fermée
Coffre clair où s'enroule mon enfance
Comme un collier désenfilé.

Je dors sur des feuilles apprivoisées
L'odeur des pins est une vieille servante aveugle
Le chant de l'eau frappe à ma tempe
Petite veine bleue rompue
Toute la rivière passe la mémoire.

Je me promène
Dans une armoire secrète.
La neige, une poignée à peine,
Fleurit sous un globe de verre
Comme une couronne de mariée.
Deux peines légères
S'étirent
Et rentrent leurs griffes.

Je vais coudre ma robe avec ce fil perdu.
J'ai des souliers bleus
Et des yeux d'enfant
Qui ne sont pas à moi.
Il faut bien vivre ici
En cet espace poli.

THE WOODEN ROOM

Time's honey
On the glistening walls
Gold ceiling
Flowers of knots
          fantastic hearts of the wood

Closed room
Bright chest where my childhood unrolls
Like an unstrung necklace.

I sleep on familiar leaves
The odor of pines is an old blind servant
The song of water beats at my temple
Small blue ruptured vein
The whole river flooding memory.

I wander
Into a secret closet.
Snow, barely a fistful,
Blossoms under a glass globe
Like a bride's crown.
Two thin pains
Stretch
And sink their claws.

I'll sew my dress with this lost thread.
I have blue shoes
And the eyes of a child
That aren't mine.
I must live here
In this polished space.

J'ai des vivres pour la nuit
Pourvu que je ne me lasse
De ce chant égal de rivière
Pourvu que cette servante tremblante
Ne laisse tomber sa charge d'odeurs
Tout d'un coup
Sans retour.

Il n'y a ni serrure ni clef ici
Je suis cernée de bois ancien.
J'aime un petit bougeoir vert.

Midi brûle aux carreaux d'argent
La place du monde flambe comme une forge
L'angoisse me fait de l'ombre
Je suis nue et toute noire sous un arbre amer.

I have provisions for the night
As long as I don't tire
Of the river's monotonous song
As long as this trembling servant
Doesn't let her burden of odor fall
All of a sudden
And forever.

There is no lock or key here
I'm surrounded by ancient wood.
I love a small green candlestick.

Noon burns in silver spaces
The square of the world flames like a forge
Anguish makes me shade
I am naked and utterly black under a bitter tree.

DE PLUS EN PLUS ÉTROIT

Cette femme à sa fenêtre
La place des coudes sur l'appui
La fureur vermeille jointe à côté
Bel arbre de capucines dans un grès bleu.

Elle regarde passer des équipages amers
Et ne bouge
De tout le jour
De peur de heurter la paroi du silence derrière elle

Souffle glacé sur sa nuque
Lieu sourd où cet homme de sel
N'a que juste l'espace
Entre cette femme de dos et le mur
Pour maudire ses veines figées à mesure qu'il respire
Sa lente froide respiration immobile.

MORE AND MORE NARROW

That woman at her window
A place for her elbows on the sill
A vermillion furor tied to her side
Lovely nasturtium in blue sandstone.

She watches a bitter traffic pass
And doesn't budge
All day
Afraid to bump into that wall of silence behind her.

Frosted breath on her neck
Silent space where that man of salt
Has just enough place
Between the woman's back and the wall
To damn her veins that freeze each time he breathes
His slow, cold and immobile breath.

UNE PETITE MORTE

Une petite morte
    s'est couchée en travers de la porte.

Nous l'avons trouvée au matin, abattue sur notre seuil
Comme un arbre de fougère plein de gel.

Nous n'osons plus sortir depuis qu'elle est là
C'est une enfant blanche dans ses jupes mousseuses
D'où rayonne une étrange nuit laiteuse.

Nous nous efforçons de vivre à l'intérieur
Sans faire de bruit
Balayer la chambre
Et ranger l'ennui
Laisser les gestes se balancer tout seuls
Au bout d'un fil invisible
A même nos veines ouvertes.

Nous menons une vie si minuscule et tranquille
Que pas un de nos mouvements lents
Ne dépasse l'envers de ce miroir limpide
Où cette sœur que nous avons
Se baigne bleue sous la lune
Tandis que croît son odeur capiteuse.

SMALL DEAD GIRL

A small dead girl
        came to stretch across our doorstep.

We found her one morning collapsed on our sill
Like a fern tree full of frost.

Now that she's there we don't dare go out
She's a white child in her mossy skirts
Glowing a strange milky darkness.

We force ourselves to live inside
Without making noise
Sweeping the room
Re-arranging boredom
Letting gestures fall all alone
At the end of the invisible thread
From our open veins.

We live such a small and tranquil life
That not one of our slow movements
Stretches beyond that limpid mirror
Where this sister that we have
Bathes herself blue in moonlight
While her heady perfume rises.

NOS MAINS AU JARDIN

Nous avons eu cette idée
De planter nos mains au jardin

Branches des dix doigts
Petits arbres d'ossements
Chère plate-bande.

Tout le jour
Nous avons attendu l'oiseau roux
Et les feuilles fraîches
A nos ongles polis.

Nul oiseau
Nul printemps
Ne se sont pris au piège de nos mains coupées.

Pour une seule fleur
Une seule minuscule étoile de couleur
Un seul vol d'aile calme
Pour une seule note pure
Répétée trois fois.

Il faudra la saison prochaine
Et nos mains fondues comme l'eau.

OUR HANDS IN THE GARDEN

We got this idea
To plant our hands in the garden.

Branches of ten fingers
Saplings of bone
Cherished rock garden.

All day long
We waited for the red bird
And the fresh leaves
Of our polished nails.

No bird
Nor spring
Was trapped in the lair of our severed hands.

For just one flower
One small star of color
The swoop of one calm wing
Just one pure note
Repeated three times

We'll need another season
And our hands must melt like water.

IL Y A CERTAINEMENT QUELQU'UN

Il y a certainement quelqu'un
Qui m'a tuée
Puis s'en est allé
Sur la pointe des pieds
Sans rompre sa danse parfaite.

A oublié de me coucher
M'a laissée debout
Toute liée
Sur le chemin
Le cœur dans son coffret ancien
Les prunelles pareilles
A leur plus pure image d'eau

A oublié d'effacer la beauté du monde
Autour de moi
A oublié de fermer mes yeux avides
Et permis leur passion perdue

SURELY SOMEONE

Surely someone
Killed me
And walked away
On tip toes
Without breaking a perfect dance.

Forgot to lay me down
Left me standing
Bound
On the road
My heart in its ancient coffer
My eyes like
Their purest image of water.

Forgot to wipe out the world's beauty
Around me
Forgot to close my starving eyes
And permits their wasted passion.

VIE DE CHATEAU

C'est un château d'ancêtres
Sans table ni feu
Ni poussière ni tapis.

L'enchantement pervers de ces lieux
Est tout dans ses miroirs polis.

La seule occupation possible ici
Consiste à se mirer jour et nuit.

Jette ton image aux fontaines dures
Ta plus dure image sans ombre ni couleur.

Vois, ces glaces sont profondes
Comme des armoires
Toujours quelque mort y habite sous le tain
Et couvre aussitôt ton reflet
Se colle à toi comme une algue

S'ajuste à toi, mince et nu,
Et simule l'amour en un lent frisson amer.

CASTLE LIFE

This is the family castle
Without a fire or table
Without carpets or dust.

The perverse enchantment of this place
Is all in its polished mirrors.

The only occupation here
Is looking into mirrors day and night.

Throw your reflection into those hard pools,
Your hardest one without shadow or color.

See, those mirrors are deep
As chests.
Some dead is always there behind the lead
And quickly covers your reflection,
Clings to you like algae,

Adjusts itself to you, thin and naked,
Counterfeiting love in a slow bitter shiver.

LE TOMBEAU DES ROIS

J'ai mon cœur au poing.
Comme un faucon aveugle.

Le taciturne oiseau pris à mes doigts
Lampe gonflée de vin et de sang,
Je descends
Vers les tombeaux des rois
Étonnée
A peine née.

Quel fil d'Ariane me mène
Au long des dédales sourds?
L'écho des pas s'y mange à mesure.

(En quel songe
Cette enfant fut-elle liée par la cheville
Pareille à une esclave fascinée?)

L'auteur du songe
Presse le fil,
Et viennent les pas nus
Un à un
Comme les premières gouttes de pluie
Au fond du puits.

Déjà l'odeur bouge en des orages gonflés
Suinte sous le pas des portes
Aux chambres secrètes et rondes,
Là où sont dressés les lits clos.

THE TOMB OF KINGS

My heart's on my fist
Like a blind falcon.

This taciturn bird gripping my fingers
Lamp swollen with wine and blood,
I go down
Toward the tomb of kings
Amazed
Barely born.

What Ariadne's thread leads me
Through the muffled labyrinths?
Echoes of footsteps swallow themselves.

(In what dream
Was this child's ankle bound
Like a spellbound slave?)

The author of the dream
Pulls the thread
And naked steps start coming
One by one
Like the first drops of rain
At the bottom of wells.

The smell already stirs in swollen storms,
Oozes under the doorsills
Into the round and secret rooms
Where the walled-in beds are raised.

L'immobile désir des gisants me tire.
Je regarde avec étonnement
A même les noirs ossements
Luire les pierres bleues incrustées.

Quelques tragédies patiemment travaillées,
Sur la poitrine des rois, couchées,
En guise de bijoux
Me sont offertes
Sans larmes ni regrets.

Sur une seule ligne rangés:
La fumée d'encens, le gâteau de riz séché
Et ma chair qui tremble:
Offrande rituelle et soumise.

Le masque d'or sur ma face absente
Des fleurs violettes en guise de prunelles,
L'ombre de l'amour me maquille à petits traits précis;
Et cet oiseau que j'ai
Respire
Et se plaint étrangement.

Un frisson long
Semblable au vent qui prend, d'arbre en arbre,
Agite sept grands pharaons d'ébène
En leurs étuis solennels et parés.

Ce n'est que la profondeur de la mort qui persiste,
Simulant le dernier tourment
Cherchant son apaisement
Et son éternité
En un cliquetis léger de bracelets
Cercles vains jeux d'ailleurs
Autour de la chair sacrifiée.

The dead's torpid desire tugs at me.
Astonished I watch
The blue encrusted stones
Shining among black bones.

A few patiently wrought tragedies
On the breasts of reclining kings
Are offered to me
Like jewels
Without regret or tears.

In one straight line:
The smoke of incense, dried rice-cakes,
And my trembling flesh:
Humble and ritual offering.

A gold mask on my absent face,
Violet flowers for my eyes,
The shadow of love, precise little lines of my make-up.
And this bird that I have
Breathes
And complains strangely.

A long shiver
Like the wind catching from tree to tree
Stirs seven great ebony Pharaohs
In their solemn decorated cases.

Only the depth of death persists,
Simulating the final agony
Seeking its appeasement
And its eternity
In a thin clash of bracelets,
Vain circles of foreign games
Around the sacrificed flesh.

Avides de la source fraternelle du mal en moi
Ils me couchent et me boivent;
Sept fois, je connais l'étau des os
Et la main sèche qui cherche le cœur pour le rompre.

Livide et repue de songe horrible
Les membres dénoués
Et les morts hors de moi, assassinés,
Quel reflet d'aube s'égare ici?
D'où vient donc que cet oiseau frémit
Et tourne vers le matin
Ses prunelles crevées?

Avid for the fraternal source of evil in me,
They lay me down and drink me:
Seven times I feel the grip of bones,
The dry hand hunting my heart to break it.

Livid and satiated with foul dreams,
My limbs freed
And the dead thrown out of me, assassinated,
What reflection of dawn wanders in here?
Why does this bird shiver
And turn toward dawn
Its gouged eyes?

Mystère
de la Parole

The Mystery
of the Word

POÉSIE, SOLITUDE ROMPUE

La poésie est une expérience profonde et mystérieuse qu'on tente en vain d'expliquer, de situer et de saisir dans sa source et son cheminement intérieur. Elle a partie liée avec la vie du poète et s'accomplit à même sa propre substance, comme sa chair et son sang. Elle appelle au fond du cœur, pareille à une vie de surcroît réclamant son droit à la parole dans la lumière. Et l'aventure singulière qui commence dans les ténèbres, à ce point sacré de la vie qui presse et force le cœur, se nomme poésie.

Parfois, l'appel vient des choses et des êtres qui existent si fortement autour du poète que toute la terre semble réclamer un rayonnement de surplus, une aventure nouvelle. Et le poète lutte avec la terre muette et il apprend la résistance de son propre cœur tranquille de muet, n'ayant de cesse qu'il n'ait trouvé une voix juste et belle pour chanter les noces de l'homme avec la terre.

Ainsi Proust, grâce au prestige de sa mémoire, délivre enfin, après une longue habitation secrète en lui, les trois clochers de Martinville qui, dès leur première rencontre avec l'écrivain, s'étaient avérés non achevés, comme en attente de cette seconde vie que la poésie peut signifier à la beauté surabondante du monde.

La poésie colore les êtres, les objets, les paysages, les sensations, d'une espèce de clarté nouvelle, particulière, qui est celle même de l'émotion du poète. Elle transplante la réalité dans une autre terre vivante qui est le cœur du poète, et cela devient une autre réalité, aussi vraie que la première. La vérité qui était éparse dans le monde prend un visage net et précis, celui d'une incarnation singulière.

Poème, musique, peinture ou sculpture, autant de moyens de donner naissance et maturité, forme et élan à cette part du monde qui vit en nous. Et je crois qu'il n'y a que la véhémence d'un très grand amour, lié à la source même du don créateur, qui puisse permettre l'œuvre d'art, la rendre efficace et durable.

POETRY: SOLITUDE BROKEN

Poetry is a profound and mysterious experience which we attempt in vain to explain, to locate, to seize at its source and in its own interior progress. It begins bound with the poet's life and grows out of his substance like his flesh and blood. It calls from the bottom of his heart like another life, reclaiming its right to the word in the light. And that singular adventure which begins in darkness, at the sacred point of life that presses and forces the heart, is called poetry.

Sometimes the call comes from things and beings existing so strongly around the poet that the whole world seems to be reclaiming an excess of light, a new adventure. And the poet struggles with the mute earth, learning the resistance of his own quiet, mute heart, but never stopping until he has found the right and beautiful voice to sing the marriage of man with the earth.

Thus, thanks to his excellent memory, after a long secret life in him Proust finally delivers the three bell-towers of Martinville which, from their first encounter with the writer, were preserved rather than lost, as if waiting for that second life which poetry can give to the world's most abundant beauty.

Poetry colors beings, objects, landscapes and sensations with a kind of new, particular light which is the poet's emotion. It transplants reality into another living ground which is the poet's heart, and that becomes another reality, as true as the first. The truth that was scattered in the world takes on a distinct and precise face, that of a singular incarnation.

Poetry, music, painting and sculpture are all means of giving birth and maturity, form and energy to that part of the world in us. And I believe that nothing but the vehemence of a great love, linked to the very source of the creative gift, can make a work of art possible, can render it effective and durable.

Tout art, à un certain niveau, devient poésie. La poésie ne s'explique pas, elle se vit. Elle est et elle remplit. Elle prend sa place comme une créature vivante et ne se rencontre que, face à face, dans le silence et la pauvreté originelle. Et le lecteur de poésie doit également demeurer attentif et démuni en face du poème, comme un tout petit enfant qui apprend sa langue maternelle. Celui qui aborde cette terre inconnue qui est l'œuvre d'un poète nouveau ne se sent-il pas dépaysé, désarmé, tel un voyageur qui, aprés avoir marché longtemps sur des routes sèches, aveuglantes de soleil, tout à coup, entre en forêt? Le changement est si brusque, la vie fraîche sous les arbres ressemble si peu au soleil dur qu'il vient de quitter, que cet homme est saisi par l'étrangeté du monde et qu'il s'abandonne à l'enchantement, subjugué par une loi nouvelle, totale et envahissante, tandis qu'il expérimente avec tous ses sens altérés, la fraîcheur exraordinaire de la forêt.

Le poème s'accomplit à ce point d'extrême tension de tout l'être créateur, habitant soudain la plénitude de l'instant, dans la joie d'être et de faire. Cet instant présent, lourd de l'expérience accumulée au cours de toute une vie antérieure, est cerné, saisi, projeté hors du temps. Par cet effort mystérieux le poète tend, de toutes ses forces, vers l'absolu, sans rien en lui qui se refuse, se ménage ou se réserve, au risque même de périr.

Mais toute œuvre, si grande soit-elle, ne garde-t-elle pas en son cœur, un manque secret, une poignante imperfection qui est le signe même de la condition humaine dont l'art demeure une des plus hautes manifestations? Rien de plus émouvant pour moi que ce signe de la terre qui blesse la beauté en plein visage et lui confère sa véritable, sensible grandeur.

L'artiste n'est pas le rival de Dieu. Il ne tente pas de refaire la création. Il demeure attentif à l'appel du don en lui. Et toute sa vie n'est qu'une longue amoureuse attention à la grâce. Il lutte avec l'ange dans la nuit. Il sait le prix du jour et de la lumière. Il apprend, à l'exemple de René Char, que «La lucidité est la blessure la plus rapprochée du soleil.»

At a certain level all art becomes poetry. Poetry can't be explained; it is lived. It is and it satisfies. It takes its place as a living creature and can be encountered only face to face, in original silence and poverty. And the reader of poetry must remain as attentive and open before a poem as a child learning his mother-tongue. And the one who reaches this unknown world, the work of a new poet, doesn't he feel strange, disarmed, like a traveler who, after having walked a long time on dry roads, blinded by sunlight, suddenly enters a forest? The change is so sudden, the coolness under the trees so unlike the hard sun he has just left, that he is seized by the strangeness of the world and abandons himself to the enchantment, subjugated by a new, total and ovewhelming law, while he experiences the extraordinary freshness of the forest with all his altered senses.

The poem occurs at that point of extreme tension of the whole creative being suddenly living the instant's fullness, in the joy of being and making. The present instant, heavy with experience accumulated in the course of a whole former life, is hemmed in, seized and projected outside of time. By this mysterious effort the poet, with all his faculties, attempts the absolute, without refusing, sparing or reserving anything of himself, even at the risk of perishing.

But doesn't any work, no matter how great, guard in its heart a secret failure, a poignant imperfection which is the very sign of the human condition, of which art remains one of the greatest manifestations? There is nothing more moving for me than this earthly sign which wounds beauty in plain sight and confers on it its true, tangible grandeur.

The artist is not God's rival. He doesn't attempt to remake creation. He remains attentive to the call of the gift in him. And his whole life is but a loving attention to grace. He wrestles with the angel in the night. He knows the price of day and light. He learns, from René Char's example, that "Lucidity is the wound closest to the sun."

Pas plus que l'araignée qui file sa toile et que la plante qui fait ses feuilles et ses fleurs, l'artiste «n'invente». Il remplit son rôle, et accomplit ce pour quoi il est au monde. Il doit se garder d'intervenir, de crainte de fausser sa vérité intérieure. Et ce n'est pas une mince affaire que de demeurer fidèle à sa plus profonde vérité, si redoutable soit-elle, de lui livrer passage et de lui donner forme. Il serait tellement plus facile et rassurant de la diriger de l'extérieur, afin de lui faire dire ce que l'on voudrait bien entendre. Et c'est à ce moment que la morale intervient dans l'art, avec toute sa rigoureuse exigence.

On a tant discuté de l'art et de la morale que le vrai problème émerge à peine d'un fatras incroyable d'idées préconçues. Selon Valéry: «Une fois la rigueur instituée, une certaine beauté est possible.» Mais la même stricte rigueur dans l'honnêteté doit être remise en question à chaque pas. Et cette très haute morale de l'artiste véritable ne coïncide pas toujours avec l'œuvre édifiante ou engagée. Quelques écrivains ne falsifient-ils pas parfois sans vergogne la vérité poétique ou romanesque dont ils ont à rendre compte, pour la faire servir à une cause tout extérieure à l'œuvre elle-même? Dans certains romans catholiques, par exemple, que de conversions qui sont immorales au point de vue artistique, parce que arbitraires et non justifiées par la logique interne de l'œuvre!

Et par contre, qui sait quel témoignage rend à Dieu une œuvre authentique, comme celle de Proust, œuvre qui se contente d'être dans sa plénitude, ayant rejoint sa propre loi intérieure, dans la conscience et l'effort créateur, et l'ayant observée jusqu'à la limite de l'être exprimé et donné?

Toute facilité est un piège. Celui qui se contente de jouer par oreille, n'ira pas très loin dans la connaissance de la musique. Et celui qui écrit des poèmes, comme on brode des mouchoirs, risque fort d'en rester là.

La poésie n'est pas le repos du septième jour. Elle agit au cœur des six premiers jours du monde, dans le tumulte de la terre et de l'eau confondus, dans l'effort de la vie qui cherche sa nourriture et son nom. Elle est soif et faim, pain et vin.

No more than the spider spinning its web or the plant making its leaves and flowers does the artist "invent." He fulfills his role and accomplishes that for which he is on earth. He must guard against interfering with, fear falsifying his inner truth. And it is no small matter to remain true to one's own most profound truth, as formidable as it may be, to allow its passage and to give it form. It would be so much simpler and reassuring to let it be determined by outside forces, in order to make it say what we'd so much like to hear. But that is the moment when morality intervenes in art, with all its rigorous demands.

Art and morality have been discussed so much that the real problem barely emerges through an incredible hodge-podge of pre-conceived ideas. As Valéry said: "Once rigor is established, a certain beauty is possible." But the same strict rigor of honesty must be questioned again at every step. And the true artist's great morality doesn't always coincide with a work that is edifying or "engagée." Don't some writers shamelessly falsify the truth of poetry or of a novel which they must account for, in order to make it serve a cause completely outside the work itself? In some Catholic novels, for example, there are conversions which are immoral from an artistic point of view because they are arbitrary and not justified by the work's own inner logic.

On the other hand, who knows what witness is rendered to God by an authentic work, like that of Proust, a work which contents itself in being its own fulness, having found its own interior law in the conscience of the artist and his effort, and having observed it to the limits of that given and expressed being?

Anything easy is a snare. Anyone who contents himself to play by ear won't go any further in acquiring a knowledge of music. And the one who writes poems as if embroidering handkerchiefs strongly risks remaining right there.

Poetry is not the rest on the seventh day. It works at the heart of the first six days of the world, in the tumult of undivided earth and water, in the struggle of life searching for its sustenance and its name. It is thirst and hunger, bread and wine.

Notre pays est à l'âge des premiers jours du monde. La vie ici est à découvrir et à nommer; ce visage obscur que nous avons, ce cœur silencieux qui est le nôtre, tous ces paysages d'avant l'homme, qui attendent d'être habités et possédés par nous, et cette parole confuse qui s'ébauche dans la nuit, tout cela appelle le jour et la lumière.

Pourtant, les premières voix de notre poésie s'élèvent déjà parmi nous. Elles nous parlent surtout de malheur et de solitude. Mais Camus n'a-t-il pas dit: «Le vrai désespoir est agonie, tombeau ou abîme, s'il parle, si'l raisonne, s'il écrit surtout, aussitôt, le frère nous tend la main, l'arbre est justifié, l'amour né. Une littérature désespérée est une contradiction dans les termes.»

Et moi, je crois à la vertu de la poésie, je crois au salut qui vient de toute parole juste, vécue et exprimée. Je crois à la solitude rompue comme du pain par la poésie.

⌒

Our country is at the age of the world's first days. Here life is to be discovered and to be named: that obscure face of ours, our silent heart, all those pre-human landscapes waiting to be inhabited and possessed by us, and this confused word roughly sketching itself in the night—all that calls for day and light.

And yet, the first voices of our poetry are already rising among us. They speak to us especially of misfortune and solitude. But didn't Camus say: "True despair is agony, the grave and the abyss; but if it speaks, if it reasons, especially if it writes, then immediately a brother extends a hand, the tree is justified, love is born. A literature of despair is a contradiction in terms."

I believe in the virtue of poetry. I believe in the salvation of all right words lived and expressed. I believe in solitude broken like bread by poetry.

MYSTÈRE DE LA PAROLE

Dans un pays tranquille nous avons reçu la passion du monde, épée nue sur nos deux mains posée

Notre cœur ignorait le jour lorsque le feu nous fut ainsi remis, et sa lumière creusa l'ombre de nos traits

C'était avant tout faiblesse, la charité seule devançant la crainte et la pudeur

Elle inventait l'univers dans la justice première et nous avions part à cette vocation dans l'extrême vitalité de notre amour

La vie et la mort en nous reçurent droit d'asile, se regardèrent avec des yeux aveugles, se touchèrent avec des mains précises

Des flèches d'odeur nous atteignirent, nous liant à la terre comme des blessures en des noces excessives

O saisons, rivière, aulnes et fougères, feuilles, fleurs, bois mouillé, herbes bleues, tout notre avoir saigne son parfum, bête odorante à notre flanc

Les couleurs et les sons nous visitèrent en masse et par petits groupes foudroyants, tandis que le songe doublait notre enchantement comme l'orage cerne le bleu de l'œil innocent

La joie se mit à crier, jeune accouchée à l'odeur sauvagine sous les joncs. Le printemps délivré fut si beau qu'il nous prit le cœur avec une seule main

Les trois coups de la création du monde sonnèrent à nos oreilles, rendus pareils aux battements de notre sang

THE MYSTERY OF THE WORD

In a peaceful country we received the passion of the world, a naked sword laid on our hands

Our hearts ignored the day when we were given fire, and its light carved the shadows of our features

That was before all weakness, charity was alone, preceding fear and shame

It invented the universe in primal justice, and in the fierce life of our love we shared in this calling

Life and death received the right of asylum in us, looking at each other with blind eyes, touching each other with keen hands

Arrows of odor hit us, pinning us to the ground like sores at expensive weddings

Oh seasons, river, alder trees and ferns, leaves, flowers, wet wood, blue grass, everything we have bleeds its fragrance, a musky beast at our flank

Colors and sounds visited us in droves and in small fiery crowds, while a dream doubled our spell like a storm surrounding an innocent blue eye

Joy began to cry out, a young woman giving birth in the savage smell among the rushes. The Spring delivered was so handsome that it grabbed our hearts with only one hand

The three blows of the world's creation rang in our ears, orchestrated like the throbbing of our blood

En un seul éblouissement l'instant fut. Son éclair nous passa sur la face et nous reçûmes mission du feu et de la brûlure.

Silence, ni ne bouge, ni ne dit, la parole se fonde, soulève notre cœur, saisit le monde en un seul geste d'orage, nous colle à son aurore comme l'écorce à son fruit

Toute la terre vivace, la forêt à notre droite, la ville profonde à notre gauche, en plein centre du verbe nous avançons à la pointe du monde

Fronts bouclés où croupit le silence en toisons musquées, toutes grimaces, vieilles têtes, joues d'enfants, amours, rides, joies, deuils, créatures, créatures, langues de feu au solstice de la terre

O mes frères les plus noirs, toutes fêtes gravées en secret; poitrines humaines, calebasses musiciennes où s'exaspèrent des voix captives

Que celui qui a reçu fonction de la parole vous prenne en charge comme un cœur ténébreux de surcroît, et n'ait de cesse que soient justifiés les vivants et les morts en un seul chant parmi l'aube et les herbes.

———

In a single dazzle the moment was. Its flare flashed over our faces, and we were given the mission of the flame and fire's scar.

Silence, nothing stirs, nothing's said, the word makes itself, lifts our hearts, seizes the world in a single stormy gesture and glues us to dawn like a peel to its fruit

The whole earth alive, the forest on our right, the dense city on our left, right in the middle of the word, we walk to the edge of the world

Foreheads where silence stagnates in musky curls, smirks, old heads, cheeks of children, loves, scars, joys, mournings, creatures, creatures, tongues of fire at the solstice of the earth

Oh my blackest brothers, all feasts secretly carved; human breasts, calabash musicians where captured voices clash

Let the one who's been given the work of the word accept you like an extra dark heart, and don't let him stop until he has justified the living and the dead in a single song at dawn among the grasses.

NAISSANCE DU PAIN

Comment faire parler le pain, ce vieux trésor tout contenu en sa stricte nécessité, pareil à un arbre d'hiver, bien attaché et dessiné, essentiel et nu, contre la transparence du jour?

Si je m'enferme avec ce nom éternel sur mon cœur, dans la chambre noire de mon recueillement, et que je presse l'antique vocable de livrer ses mouvantes images,

J'entends battre contre la porte, lâches et soumises, mille bêtes aigres au pelage terne, aux yeux aveugles; toute une meute servile qui mâchonne des mots comme des herbes depuis les aubes les plus vieilles.

Qu'en ce cœur véhément du poète s'étende donc le clair espace balayé, le long champ de solitude et de dénuement, tandis qu'à l'horizon délivré poindra parmi les âges décelés, comme de plates pierres bleues sous la mer, le goût du pain, du sel et de l'eau, à même la faim millénaire.

Soudain la faim déliée s'agenouille sur la terre, y plante son cœur rond comme un lourd sommeil.

O la longue première nuit, la face contre le sol craquelé, épiant le battement du sang donné, tout songe banni, tout mouvement retenu, toute attention gonflée au point le plus haut de l'amour.

Le chaume cru crève la campagne, la vie souterraine laisse percer sa chevelure verte. Le ventre de la terre découvre ses fleurs et ses fruits au grand soleil de midi.

L'azur poudroie comme une poussière d'eau; nos mains peintes au ras du champ deviennent pareilles à de grands pavots clairs.

THE BIRTH OF BREAD

How can I make bread speak, this ancient treasure wholly held in its own strict necessity, like a tree in winter, precisely outlined and tied down, essential and naked against the transparence of day?

If I lock myself up with this eternal name in my heart in the black room of my meditation, and if I force this ancient word to deliver its moving images,

I hear a thousand peevish beasts, cowardly and tame, with dull fur and blind eyes, beating against my door; a whole cringing pack munching words like grass from ancient dawns.

Let a clean swept space open in the poet's vehement heart, a wide field of loneliness and nakedness, while on the freed horizon, among the ages betrayed like flat blue rocks under the sea, the taste for bread, for salt and water will sprout out of a century's famine.

Suddenly hunger, set free, kneels on the ground and plants its round heart like a heavy sleep.

O that long first night, face against the parched earth, spying on the throbbing of the given blood, all dreams banished, all movement checked, all attention swollen to love's breaking point.

The raw stubble pierces the countryside, a subterranean life lets its green hair grow. The earth's belly bares its flowers and fruits to the sun at high noon.

Azure crumbles into powder like spindrift; our painted hands level with the field open like bright huge poppies.

Toute forme et couleur provoquées montent de la terre telles une respiration visible et rythmée.

Le champ palpite et moutonne, toison blanchissante sous l'éclat strident de l'été aux cigales acides.

Les meules grenues et poreuses ont l'ardeur sourde des grands miroirs opaques et condamnés.

Il n'est que de servir dans l'ombre, d'être pesantes et ténébreuses, mauvaises, dures et grincantes, pour briser le cœur de la moisson, de le réduire en poussière comme un averse sèche et étouffante.

D'étranges coquillages aigus et chantants, vives fleurs d'eau que le soleil marin cristallise et foudroie s'ouvrent à l'instant pour nous en des formes profondes et travaillées.

Nous y lisserons la pâte laiteuse, plate et molle, toute l'œuvre couchée, étale et roulée à qui le souffle manque encore et qui dort comme un étang.

Si d'aventure le vent se levait, si de ferveur notre âme se donnait toute, avec sa nuit chargée de racines et trouée par le jour?

Sous la cendre qui se défait comme un lit, voici la miche et le chanteau rebondis, la profonde chaleur animale et ce cœur impalpable, bien au centre, comme un oiseau captif.

Ah nous sommes vivants, et le jour recommence à l'horizon! Dieu peut naître à son tour, enfant blême, au bord des saisons mis en croix; notre œuvre est déjà levée, colorée et poignante d'odeur!

Nous lui offrons du pain pour sa faim.

All shapes and colors called rise from the earth like a visible and rhythmic breath.

The field throbs and froths, fleece whitening under the summer's strident flash of acid cicadas.

Grained and porous millstones have the dull glow of huge, opaque and condemned mirrors.

There's nothing to do but serve in the shade, be heavy and dark, evil, hard and grinding, to break the heart of the harvest, reduce it to dust like a dry and stifling downpour.

Strange shells, shrill and singing, bright flowers of water crystallized and blasted by the watery sun, at that moment open for us in thick, wrought shapes.

We'll make the milky pulp smooth, flat and soft, the whole work laid out, flattened, rolled, still breathless and sleeping like a pond.

What if the wind should accidently rise, what if out of zeal our soul should give itself completely, with its night loaded with roots and punctured by day?

Among the cinders unmaking themselves like beds, see the plump loaf and the chunk rise, the fierce animal heat and this impalpable heart at its very center like a captive bird.

Ah, we're alive, and day begins again on the horizon! God could take his turn to be born, pale child on the edge of the crossed seasons: our work has already risen, colored and gripping with odor!

We offer him bread for his hunger.

Et nous allons dormir, créatures lourdes, marquées de fête et d'ivresse que l'aube surprend, tout debout en travers du monde.

Il y viendrait par surcroît cette âpre mesure de notre plus vieille mort, macérée comme les feuilles d'octobre aux senteurs fauves, en guise de levain.

Parmi la fumée des chairs brûlées, sur la pierre noircie, parmi les festins sauvages renversés, voici que s'allume dans la nuit primitive une pure vielleuse et que commence cette lente maturité de la croûte et de la mie, tandis que la Patience s'assoit sur la margelle du feu.

Et nul n'a accès à son silence jusqu'au matin.

And we'll sleep, heavy creatures marked by intoxicating joy that dawn surprises, straddling the earth.

Out of that surplus would come this harsh measure of our oldest death, macerated like wild smelling October leaves, instead of leaven.

In the smoke of burnt flesh, on the blackened stone, among the overturned savage banquets, in the primitive night a pure vigil light is lit and the slow growth of the crust and pulp begins, while Patience sits at the fire's edge.

And no one can reach her silence until dawn.

ALCHIMIE DU JOUR

Qu'aucune servante ne te serve en ce jour où tu lias ta peine sauvage, bête de sang aux branches basses du noir sapin,

Ne le dites pas aux filles de feux roux, ne prévenez pas les filles aux cœurs violets;

Elles paraîtraient toutes les sept en ta chambre portant les pitiés bleues en des amphores tranquilles hissées sur leurs cheveux,

Elles glisseraient la longue file de leurs ombres mauves pareilles à l'envers des flammes marines en une calme frise processionnelle aux quatre vents de tes murs.

Ne prévenez pas les filles aux pieds de feutre vert découpés à même d'antiques tapis réservés au déroulement lent des douleurs sacrées, pré doux au soleil tondu, aux herbes silencieuses et drues sans l'espace vif du cri,

Ni l'obscure et forte vibration de l'amour souterrain semblable à la passion excessive de la mer en l'origine de son chant appareillant.

La première fille alertée joindrait ses sœurs, une à une, et leur parlerait bas de l'amour blessé amarré aux feuillages de tes veines ouvertes,

La plus sombre des sœurs désignées te porterait des baumes nouvellement fleuris sur des cœurs amers, très vieux celliers désaffectés, plate-bande des remèdes et des conseils nocturnes,

Tandis que la plus lente d'entre elles referait son visage de larmes brûlées comme une belle pierre mise à jour sous des fouilles patientes et pures,

THE ALCHEMY OF DAY

Let no servant wait on you that day when you bind your wild wounds, bloody beast, to the black pine's low branches.

Don't tell the girls around the rusty fire, don't warn the girls with violet hearts.

All seven of them will appear in your room carrying blue pities in quiet amphoras hoisted on their hair.

They'll slide along the thread of their shadows, mauve like the back of underwater flames, in a calm processional freize along the four winds of your walls.

Don't warn the girls with green felt feet cut out of antique rugs reserved for the slow unrolling of sacred sorrows, soft meadows mowed by the sun, silent and thick grass without the cry's stark space,

Nor the hidden strong vibration of an underground love like the excessive passion of the sea at the start of a sailing song.

The first girl alerted will gather her sisters one by one and tell them softly about the wounded lover moored in the leaves of your open veins.

The darkest of those appointed sisters will bring you balsam just blossomed out of bitter hearts, old desecrated cellars, flower beds of medicine and midnight diagnoses.

While the slowest will remake her face of burnt tears like a lovely stone brought to light by patient and precise excavations.

La voici qui délègue vers toi une fille de sel portant des paniers fins pour ses moissons claires. Elle soupèse en chemin le poids de tes pleurs cueillis à la pointe de l'ongle comme la rosée sur le jardin qui s'affale,

Vois, celle qui a nom Véronique plie de grandes toiles pures et rêve d'un visage à saisir en sa grimace à même des voiles déroulées comme de clairs miroirs d'eau,

Se hâte la fille-fièvre parée d'épines cuivrées, maintenant que la nuit, en sa haute taille levée, bouge ses paumes mûres comme de noirs tournesols,

Sur tes paupières bientôt elle posera ses mains étroitement comme des huîtres vives où la mort médite, des siècles de songe sans faille, la blanche floraison d'une perle dure.

O toi qui trembles dans le vent, ayant hissé la beauté de ton visage au mât des quatre saisons,

Toi qui grinces de sable, ointe par des huiles pures, nue, en des miracles certains de couleur agile et d'eau puissante,

Redoute l'avènement silencieux des compassions crayeuses aux faces d'argiles brouillés;

Pose le vert contre le bleu, usant d'un vif pouvoir, ne crains pas l'ocre sur le pourpre, laisse débonder le verbe se liant au monde telle la flèche à son arc,

Laisse le don alerté mûrir son étrange alchimie en des équipages fougueux,

Profère des choses sauvages dans le soleil, nomme toute chose face au tumulte des grands morts friables et irrités.

See, she delegates a girl of salt to bring you gorgeous baskets for her bright harvest. On the way she weighs your tears like dew plucked off a sinking garden with the tips of fingernails.

See, the one called Veronica folds large pure sheets and dreams of trapping a tortured face in her veils unrolled like clear mirrors of water.

The feverish girl stuck with brass thorns hurries now that night, risen to its full height, stirs its ripe palms like black sunflowers.

Soon she'll lay her hands tightly on your eyelids like live oysters where death meditates, centuries of perfect dreams, the white bloom of a hard pearl.

O you trembling in the wind, the beauty of your face hoisted on the four seasons' mast,

You grating with sand, annointed with pure oils, naked in sure miracles of agile color and powerful water,

Beware of the silent coming of chalk compassions with faces of mixed clays.

Poise the green against the blue, and, possessor of power, don't be afraid of ochre and purple, let the word rush out bound to the world like an arrow to its arc.

Let the alerted gift ripen its strange alchemy in impetuous traffic,

Utter wild things in the sun, name everything facing the tumult of the great crumbling and irritated dead.

Les murs aux tessons bleus crèvent comme des cercles d'eau sur la mer,

Et le point du cœur dessine sa propre souple ceinture,

Le jour, pour la seconde fois convoqué, monte en parole comme un large pavot éclatant sur sa tige.

The walls of broken blue glass break like circles of water in the sea,

And the heart's very center designs its own supple fence.

Called for a second time, day rises on the word like a huge poppy exploding on its stem.

JE SUIS LA TERRE ET L'EAU

Je suis la terre et l'eau, tu ne me passeras pas à gué, mon ami, mon ami

Je suis le puits et la soif, tu ne me traverseras pas sans péril, mon ami, mon ami

Midi est fait pour crever sur la mer, soleil étale, parole fondue, tu étais si clair, mon ami, mon ami

Tu ne me quitteras pas essuyant l'ombre sur ta face comme un vent fugace, mon ami, mon ami

Le malheur et l'espérance sous mon toit brûlent, durement noués, apprends ces vieilles noces étranges, mon ami, mon ami

Tu fuis les présages et presses le chiffre pur à même tes mains ouvertes, mon ami, mon ami

Tu parles à haute et intelligible voix, je ne sais quel écho sourd traîne derrière toi, entends, entends mes veines noires qui chantent dans la nuit, mon ami, mon ami

Je suis sans nom ni visage certain; lieu d'accueil et chambre d'ombre, piste de songe et lieu d'origine, mon ami, mon ami

Ah quelle saison d'âcres feuilles rousses m'a donnée Dieu pour t'y coucher, mon ami, mon ami

Un grand cheval noir court sur les grèves, j'entends son pas sous la terre, son sabot frappe la source de mon sang à la fine jointure de la mort

I AM EARTH AND WATER

I am earth and water, you won't wade through me, my friend, my friend

I am the well and thirst, you won't cross me without danger, my friend, my friend

Noon is set to explode on the sea, slack sun, melted word, you were so bright, my friend, my friend

You won't abandon me while wiping shade from your face like a fleeting wind, my friend, my friend

Misery and hope burn under my roof, knotted tight, learn these strange ancient marriages, my friend, my friend

You flee omens and press pure signs across your open hands, my friend, my friend

You speak in a high, clear voice, I don't know what vague echo drags behind you, listen to my black veins singing in the night, my friend, my friend

I have no specific name or face, no resting place or shaded room, path for dreams or birthplace, my friend, my friend

Ah what bitter season of rusty leaves did God give me to lay with you, my friend, my friend

A huge black horse runs on the beach, I hear him galloping underground, his hoof raps the spring of my blood at that fine joint of death

Ah quel automne! Qui donc m'a prise parmi des cheminements de fougères souterraines, confondue à l'odeur du bois mouillé, mon ami, mon ami

Parmi les âges brouillés, naissances et morts, toutes mémoires, couleurs rompues, reçois le cœur obscur de la terre, toute la nuit entre tes mains livrée et donnée, mon ami, mon ami

Il a suffi d'un seul matin pour que mon visage fleurisse, reconnais ta propre grande ténèbre visitée, tout le mystère lié entre tes mains claires, mon amour.

What a Fall! Who took me on my wanderings around the subterranean ferns, mixed with the smell of wet wood, my friend, my friend

Among the misty ages, births and deaths, all memories, broken colors, receive the mysterious heart of the earth, the whole night surrendered and put in your hands, my friend, my friend

Only one morning sufficed for my face to bloom, to recognize your own great visited night, the whole mystery bound in your bright hands, my love.

LA SAGESSE M'A ROMPU LES BRAS

La sagesse m'a rompu les bras, brisé les os
C'était une très vieille femme envieuse
Pleine d'onction, de fiel et d'eau verte

Elle m'a jeté ses douceurs à la face
Désirant effacer mes traits comme une image mouillée
Lissant ma colère comme une chevelure noyée

Et moi j'ai crié sous l'insulte fade
Et j'ai réclamé le fer et le feu de mon héritage.

Voulant y faire pousser son âme bénie comme une vigne
Elle avait taillé sa place entre mes côtes.
Longtemps son parfum m'empoisonna des pieds à la tête

Mais l'orage mûrissait sous mes aisselles,
Musc et feuilles brûlées,
J'ai arraché la sagesse de ma poitrine,
Je l'ai mangée par les racines,
Trouvée amère et crachée comme un noyau pourri

J'ai rappelé l'ami le plus cruel, la ville l'ayant chassé, les mains
    pleines de pierres.
Je me suis mise avec lui pour mourir sur des grèves mûres
O mon amour, fourbis l'éclair de ton cœur, nous nous battrons
    jusqu'à l'aube
La violence nous dresse en de très hautes futaies
Nos richesses sont profondes et noires pareilles au contenu des
    mines que l'éclair foudroie.

WISDOM BROKE MY ARMS

Wisdom broke my arms, factured my bones
It was a very old and envious woman
Full of unction, gall and green water

She threw her sweetness in my face
Hoping to erase my features like a wet picture
Smoothing my anger like drowned hair

And I screamed under her faded insult
And I reclaimed the steel and fire of my heritage.

Hoping to make her blessed soul grow like a vine
She dug a place for herself between my ribs
Her perfume poisoned me from head to foot for a long time.

But the storm ripened in my armpits,
Musk and burnt leaves,
I tore wisdom from my breast,
I ate it by the roots,
Found it bitter and spat it out like a rotten pit.

I called back my cruellest friend, chased out by the city, hands
     full of rocks.
I got together with him to die on consummate shores.
Oh my love, polish your shining heart, we'll fight until dawn
Violence lifts us up like fully grown trees
Our wealth is great and black like ore in mines blown up by
     lightning.

En route, voici le jour, fièvre en plein cœur scellée
Des chants de coqs trouent la nuit comme des lueurs
Le soleil appareille à peine, déjà sûr de son plein midi,
Tout feu, toutes flèches, tout désir au plus vif de la lumière,
Envers, endroit, amour et haine, toute la vie en un seul
    honneur.

Des chemins durs s'ouvrent à perte de vue sans ombrage
Et la ville blanche derrière nous lave son seuil où coucha la
    nuit.

Now let's go, day's on its way, a fever sealed in its heart
The crow of roosters splits the night like a flash
The sun barely shines, already sure of its high noon,
All fire, all shafts, all desire in the brightest light,
Wrong side, right side, love and hate, all life in just one honor.

Hard roads open up without shade as far as the eye can see,
And the white city behind us washes its threshold where night
    slept.

LA VILLE TUÉE

Le sel et l'huile purifièrent également la ville, l'eau n'étant point sûre et le recours à Dieu périmé

On étancha le marais, l'oiseau de proie fut capturé, toutes ailes déployées, le plus doux d'entre nous assura qu'il le ferait dormir en croix sur la porte

La veille déjà, toute larme, mal, peur, songe ou pitié avaient été chassés

L'horreur de la mort nous guidant, certaines images jugées maléfiques sur-le-champ furent interdites

La main droite de chacun fut posée à plat sur le ciel afin de vérifier chaque jointure et la précision des os dans la lumière

Un instant on songea à l'éclat du feu pour éprouver quelques visages trop fins, la crainte de l'incendie dans la chevelure du bourreau empêcha seule ce sacrifice.

Les enfants furent endormis de force sans bruit

On érigea le dogme et la morale, et la première saison s'allongea sans passion

Un vent lourd s'abattit sur toutes choses. C'était le jugement au comble de lui-même croissant sur nous, régnant à perte de vue

Les souvenirs furent passés au crible, tout amour impitoyablement saisi avec toute mémoire rêveuse ou insolente

Longtemps la douleur et la mort semblèrent subjugués. Cela fit un beau pays sec pour s'étendre et faire le guet

THE MURDERED CITY

Salt and oil purified the city just as well, since water wasn't safe and recourse to God outdated

We drained the marsh, captured the bird of prey, all wings spread, the most gentle of us swearing he'd put it to sleep, a cross on the door

Of course, the night before, all tears, pain, fear, dream or pity had been purged

The horror of death guiding us, certain images judged malevolent were forbidden at once

Everyone's right hand was flattened against the sky to verify each joint and the bones' precision in the light

For a moment we considered the flash of fire to test certain faces that were too fine, only the fear of fire in the executioner's hair prevented this sacrifice

The children were put to sleep by force, noiselessly.

We erected dogma and morals, and the first season lengthened without passion

A heavy wind crashed down on everything. It was judgment at its own peak growing over us, reigning everywhere

Memories were sifted, all love ruthlessly seized along with all dreamy or insolent memory

For a long time suffering and death seemed conquered. That was a lovely dry country to lie in, watching

Bientôt l'ennui fleurit par petites places vertes et risque de
devenir plaie et gangrène

La plus jeune, affichant son deuil, hissa l'angoisse aux yeux de
tous, sur le plus haut mur qui regarde la terre

Le désir de l'eau devint si amer que les larmes furent invoquées
comme un bien

La fille cria qu'elle n'avait ni cœur ni visage et qu'on l'avait trahie
dès l'origine

Hors les murs chassée, tardant à fleurir, abrupte comme la soif
sur son aire, elle se retourna

Derrière elle la ville s'effritait, pierres, sable, cendres, fleurs de
pavots, cœurs vermeils dans le vent

L'effroi dans ses veines, la pitié entre ses mains, la fille éprouva
d'un coup le malheur du monde en sa chair

Et découvrit son propre tendre visage éclatant parmi les larmes.

Soon boredom bloomed in small green places and threatened to become a wound and gangrene

The youngest girl, brandishing her mourning, hoisted agony up on the highest wall overlooking the earth for all to see

The lust for water became so bitter that tears were invoked as a blessing

The girl screamed that she had neither a heart nor a face and that we'd betrayed her from the start

Chased outside the city walls, late to bloom, abrupt as thirst in her eyrie, she turned around

Behind her the city crumbled, stones, sand, cinders, petals of poppies, vermillion hearts in the wind

Fear in her veins, pity between her hands, in one stroke the girl tested the world's misfortune in her flesh

And discovered her own tender face exploding among tears.

TROP A L'ÉTROIT

Trop à l'étroit dans le malheur, l'ayant crevé comme une vieille peau

Vieille tunique craque aux coutures, se déchire et se fend de bas en haut

L'ayant habité à sueur et à sang, vétuste caverne où s'ébrèche l'ombre du soleil

Ayant épuisé de tristes amours, la vie en rond, le cœur sans levain

Nous sommes réveillés un matin, nus et seuls sur la pierre de feu

Et la beauté du jour nous trouva sans défense, si vulnérables et doux de larmes

Qu'aussitôt elle nous coucha en joue comme des fusillés tranquilles.

TOO CRAMPED

Too cramped by misfortune, we tore it like an old skin

An old coat split at the seams, torn and ripped from top to bottom

Having lived in it in sweat and blood, decrepit cavern where the sun's shadow's chipped

Having drained dreary loves, life's refrain, the heart without yeast

We woke up one morning, naked and alone on the fire stone

And the day's beauty found us so defenseless, so vulnerable and soft with tears

That right away it shot at us like passive victims of a firing squad.

ÈVE

Reine et maîtresse certaine crucifiée aux portes de la ville la plus lointaine

Effraie rousse aux ailes clouées, toute jointure disjointe, toute envergure fixée

Chair acide des pommes vertes, beau verger juteux, te voici dévastée claquant dans le vent comme un drapeau crevé

Fin nez de rapace, bec de corne, nous nous en ferons des amulettes aux jours de peste

Contre la mort, contre la rage, nous te porterons scapulaires de plumes et d'os broyés

Femme couchée, grande fourmilière sous le mélèze, terre antique criblée d'amants

Nous t'invoquons, ventre premier, fin visage d'aube passant entre les côtes de l'homme la dure barrière du jour

Vois tes fils et tes époux pourrissent pêle-mêle entre tes cuisses, sous une seule malédiction

Mère du Christ souviens-toi des filles dernière-nées, de celles qui sont sans nom ni histoire, tout de suite fracassées entre deux très grandes pierres

Source des larmes et du cri, de quelles parures vives nous léguas-tu la charge et l'honneur. L'angoisse et l'amour, le deuil et la joie se célèbrent à fêtes égales, en pleine face gravées, comme des paysages profonds

EVE

Absolute queen and mistress crucified at the gates of the farthest city,

Russet screech-owl with nailed wings, all joints disjointed, wing-spread fixed,

Acid flesh of green apples, gorgeous juicy orchard, here you are devastated and flapping in the wind like a torn flag.

From your rapacious nose, your beak of horn, we'll make amulets for ourselves against the days of plague,

Against death, against rage we'll wear you, scapulars of feathers and ground bones.

Sleeping woman, huge ant hill under the larch, antique earth riddled with lovers,

We invoke you, first womb, fine face of dawn passing between man's ribs, day's hard barrier;

Look, your sons and husbands are rotting at random between your thighs, under only one curse.

Mother of Christ, remember your last-born daughters, those without name or history, soon crushed between two huge rocks.

Source of tears and the cry, for what living ornament did you will us the charge and the honor. Anguish and love, mourning and joy are equally celebrated feasts, engraved on our face like thick landscapes.

Mère aveugle, explique-nous la naissance et la mort et tout le voyage hardi entre deux barbares ténèbres, pôles du monde, axes du jour

Dis-nous le maléfice et l'envoûtement de l'arbre, raconte-nous le jardin, Dieu clair et nu et le péché farouchement désiré comme l'ombre en plein midi

Dis-nous l'amour sans défaut et le premier homme défait entre tes bras

Souviens-toi du cœur initial sous le sacre du matin, et renouvelle notre visage comme un destin pacifié

La guerre déploie ses chemins d'épouvante, l'horreur et la mort se tiennent la main, liés par des secrets identiques, les quatre éléments bardés d'orage se lèvent pareils à des dieux sauvages offensés

La douceur sous le fer est brûlée jusqu'à l'os, son cri transperce l'innocent et le coupable sur une seule lame embrochés

Vois-nous, reconnais-nous, fixe sur nous ton regard sans prunelle, considère l'aventure de nos mains filant le mystère à la veillée comme une laine rude

L'enfant à notre sein roucoule, l'homme sent le pain brûlé, et le milieu du jour se referme sur nous comme une eau sans couture

Ève, Ève, nous t'appelons du fond de cette paix soudaine comme si nous nous tenions sans peine sur l'appui de notre cœur justifié

Que ta mémoire se brise au soleil, et, au risque de réveiller le crime endormi, retrouve l'ombre de la grâce sur ta face comme un rayon noir.

Blind mother, explain birth and death to us, and the whole bold journey between two barbarous nights, pole of the world, axes of the day.

Tell us about the bewitching magic of the tree, tell us about the garden, God bright and naked, and the sin so fiercely wished for like shade at high noon.

Tell us about love without fault and the first man undone in your arms.

Remember the first heart in the rite of morning and renew our faces like an appeased destiny.

War unrolls its road of terror, horror and death hold hands, bound by identical secrets, and the four elements barded with storms rise like offended savage gods.

The softness under the iron is burned to the bone, its cry pierces the innocent and guilty skewered on the same sword.

See us, recognize us, fix your eyeless stare on us, consider the adventure of our hands spinning mystery all night like raw wool.

The child at our breast coos, the man smells the bread burning, and the center of the day collapses on us like water without seams.

Eve, Eve, we call to you from the depths of this sudden peace as if we held ourselves up easily on the prop of our justified heart.

Let memory shatter itself in the sun and, at the risk of reawakening the sleeping crime, rediscover the shade of grace on your face like a black beam.

DES DIEUX CAPTIFS

Des dieux captifs ayant mis en doute le bien-fondé de nos visions

Nous prédisant la fin du monde depuis l'apogée des mûres saisons

Nous décidâmes par des chemins de haut mystère de les mener au bord de l'horizon

Le ciel, le feu, la terre et l'eau ayant macéré ensemble durant des noces millénaires

Il n'en subsistait qu'une mince ligne bleue difficile à saisir sans éblouissement

Comme si toute la vie eût été cachée sous l'eau de pluie, contre le soleil à midi

Notre désir d'appréhender la source du monde en son visage brouillé

Depuis longtemps nous ravageait l'âme pareil à des brûlures hautes dans un ciel barbare

Le bleu s'étant accumulé en ce lieu, par instants il tournait au vert et déjà le violet éclatait de-ci de-là, liquide et fort

Si près, si près de ce cœur défait nous respirâmes la grande libre couleur exaltante et cruelle, absolu de l'air marin avant qu'il n'éclate en trombe

Dans un coin la nudité des morts parés de blessures profondes luisait, rendue belle par le seul éclatement de leurs songes

CAPTIVE GODS

Having threatened the validity of our visions, captive gods

Predicted the end of the world at the climax of ripe seasons

Through the ways of high mystery we decided to lead them to the edge of the horizon

The sky, fire, earth and water fused together during millenial weddings

Nothing survived but a thin blue line hard to seize without being blinded

As if all life had been hidden under the water of rain, against the noon sun

Our desire to seize the source of the world with its blurred face

Ravaged our soul for a long time like burning wounds high in a barbaric sky

Blue accumulated in this place, now and then turned to green, and even violet flashed here and there, liquid and strong

So close, so close to this exhausted heart we breathed the great, free, exalting and cruel color, absolute of the sea air before it explodes into whirlwind

In a corner the nakedness of corpses adorned with deep wounds glowed, made lovely by the very burst of their dreams

Tout semblait définitif, calme prairie marine. Mais tant de sœurs vives au large rayonnaient pareilles à des bancs de capucines

Que s'éveillèrent les dieux amers qu'on traînait avec soi, cavalcade souterraine, sabots de justice, envoûtement, tournent nos cœurs entre nos doigts, manèges, fleurs écarlates convoitées

Un seul bouquet de mûres a suffi pour teindre la face des dieux, masque de sang; voici nos sœurs désirées comme la couleur-mère du monde

La vie est remise en marche, l'eau se rompt comme du pain, roulent les flots, s'enluminent les morts et les augures, la marée se fend à l'horizon, se brise la distance entre nos sœurs et l'aurore debout sur son glaive.

Incarnation, nos dieux tremblent avec nous! La terre se fonde à nouveau, voici l'image habitable comme une ville et l'honneur du poète lui faisant face, sans aucune magie: dure passion.

Everything seemed final, calm prairie of water. But there were so many vibrant sisters at large glowing like banks of nasturtiums

That the bitter gods we dragged with us awoke, subterranean cavalcade, clogs of justice, spell, turning our hearts between our fingers, carousels, coveted scarlet flowers

Only one bouquet of mulberry sufficed to dye the face of the gods, mask of blood; now our sisters are desired like the mother-color of the world

Life sets out again, water breaks like bread, waves roll, corpses and omens are lit, the sea splits on the horizon, the distance between our sisters and dawn standing on its sword is broken.

Incarnation, our gods tremble with us! The earth begins again, here is an image as inhabitable as a city, the honor of the poet face to face with it, no magic at all: hard passion.

Poèmes
Inédits

Uncollected
Poems

LES OFFENSÉS

Par ordre de famine les indigents furent alignés
Par ordre de colère les séditieux furent examinés
Par ordre de bonne conscience les maîtres furent jugés
Par ordre d'offense les humiliés furent questionnés
Par ordre de blessure les crucifiés furent considérés
En cette misère extrême les muets venaient en tête
Tout un peuple de muets se tenait sur les barricades
Leur désir de parole était si urgent
Que le Verbe vint à leur rencontre de par les rues
Le faix dont on le chargea fut si lourd
Que le cri «feu» lui éclata du cœur
En guise de parole.

THE OFFENDED

The poor were lined up in famine's order
The seditious were examined in anger's order
The masters were judged in good conscience's order
The humiliated were interrogated in offense's order
The crucified were considered in mutilation's order
In this extreme misery the mutes came to the front lines
A whole nation of mutes stayed on the barricades
Their desire for the word was so urgent
That the Verb came through the streets to meet them
The burden it was charged with was so heavy
That the cry "fire" exploded from its heart
Disguised as a word.

VILLES EN MARCHE

Villes en marche sur l'eau, places de sel, nénuphars de pierre

Iles dévalant les pentes de mer, vent debout, soleil en proue

Bouquets amers hissés sur la vague, lumière géranium aux crêtes des coqs verts rangés

Marchement d'eaux, remue-ménage de soleil, retombées soudaines de manteaux saumâtres, nuit, pleine nuit

Cortège de haute mer revenu, le port comme une étoile, lit ouvert crissant le goémon et le zeste

Barques amarrées, balancées, jour en berne, cœur étalé parmi les algues

Paumes ouvertes, d'étranges ibis très bleus vont y boire en silence

Toute la douceur respire largement alentour. La terre entière s'est apprivoisée.

CITIES SETTING OUT

Cities setting out on the water, salt squares, stone water-lilies,

Islands racing down slopes of the sea, head-wind, sun at the prow,

Bitter bouquets hoisted on the wave, geranium light on rows of green cockscombs,

The march of waters, bustle of the sun, the sudden fall of brackish cloaks, night, dead of night,

Cortege come back from the high sea, port like a star, open bed grinding seaweed and rind,

Boats moored, balanced, day at half-mast, the heart layed out among algae,

Open palms where very blue, strange ibis go to drink in silence,

All around, total tenderness breathes deeply. The whole earth has tamed itself.

COURONNE DE FÉLICITÉ

La mort en louve morte changée
Cadavre pierreux à l'horizon brûlé

Le rêve petites fumées de village
Fument cent maisons dos à dos

Les dormeurs nagent dans une nuit sans étage
Fleurant l'algue et la mer

Ton visage lumière
Eveil
La vie d'un trait
L'amour d'un souffle

Le jour recommence
La nuit passe la ligne des eaux
L'aube toutes ailes déployées
Illumine la terre

La joie à bout de bras
Le poème au sommet de la tête hissé
Couronne de félicité

CROWN OF JOY

Death changed into a dead she-wolf
Rocky cadaver on the burnt horizon

The dream frail smoke of the village
A hundred houses smoking back to back

The sleepers swim in a tierless night
Smelling of algae and sea

Your face light
Awakens
Life in one draught
Love in one breath

Day begins again
Night crosses the line of waters
All wings deployed dawn
Illumines the earth

Happiness at arm's length
The poem at the summit of the hoisted head
Crown of joy

FIN DU MONDE

Je suis le cri et la blessure, je suis la femme à ton flanc qu'on outrage et qu'on viole.

L'Apocalypse t'enchaîne à son char, l'horreur te lie les mains, amour, amour qui t'a crevé les yeux?

Mon cœur de paix violente, je te l'avais donné, plus nu que mon corps,

J'ai des caresses ruisselantes, la mort et les larmes sont mes parures,

Mon âme, sous un feu si noir, sèche comme le sel, et ta soif s'y pose, bel oiseau fou.

Amour, amour; ni pain, ni jour, la terre flambe, l'éclair s'étend entre nous, malédiction!

Le feu lâché, bête infinie, l'âge de la terre se rompt par le milieu,

Tout l'horizon, bel anneau bleu, d'un seul coup, se raye à jamais, ceinture de roc tordue. Passé, avenir abolis, règne le présent, vaste empire des furies; l'agonie du monde se fonde, démence au poing.

Au centre de la femme germent l'ange-poisson, la licorne aveugle, et mille fougères bistres, pour fleurir de vastes plaines sans air, ni eau, absence aux crosses brûlées,

Toute enfance annulée, notre fils, comme du sable, file entre nos doigts,

END OF THE WORLD

I am the cry and the wound, I am the outraged and violated woman at your side.

The Apocalypse chains you to its chariot, horror ties your hands, love, love, who gouged your eyes?

My heart of violent peace, I had given it to you, more naked than my body,

My caresses flow, death and tears are my jewelry,

Under such a black fire, my soul dries up like salt, and your thirst perches on it, lovely wild bird.

Love, love; neither bread nor day, the earth flares, lightning stretches itself between us, a curse!

The fire launched, timeless beast, the age of the earth splits open at its center,

With just one blow the whole horizon, lovely blue ring, scores itself out forever, belt of twisted rock. Past, future abolished, the present rules, vast empire of furies; the world's agony melts, madness in hand.

At the woman's center the angel-fish, the blind unicorn and a thousand swarthy ferns germinate to flower vast plains without air or water, absence of burned staves,

All childhood annulled, our son trickles through our fingers like sand,

Souviens-toi. Encore un peu, souviens-toi; nos mains jointes ensemble. Souviens-toi! L'injustice roule un flot de boue. Tendre mémoire craque à nos tempes.

Tes yeux, tes yeux sur moi, le ciel se déchire de haut en bas, l'effroi dessine un tableau vide,

La fièvre court en ce désert, tremble la terre, vielle échine broyée.

Tes mains, tes mains sur mon cœur, encore un peu de temps, un peu de temps, folle prière,

Le sang dans tes veines fait des bonds terribles, se change en monstre, toute fureur moquée, entends ce rire énorme secouer mille forêts abattues,

Ta bouche sur la mienne, viennent la poussière et la cendre; amour, amour perdu.

Haine et guerre, souviens-toi, souviens-toi, amour blessé, quelle longue jarre fraîche à ton flanc renversée, c'était l'été.

Grondent les hivers noirs amassés; ta force, ta force ami, qui t'a désarmé, te prennent le cœur comme une fronde?

Et toi et moi, et moi et toi, et toi avec moi! Vivre! Nous sortirons de ce puits, la mort n'a pas si grand visage qu'elle barre l'entrée jamais.

Le silence pousse dans ma bouche comme une herbe. Tous les mots, un jour, me furent livrés. Ne trouve que ce cri.

Maison pillée. Cœur ouvert. Dernière saison. Plus que ce cri en plein ventre. Fontaine de sang. Cri. Qui te rappelle en vain, amour, amour tué.

Remember. Remember still a little more; our hands joined together. Remember! Injustice rides a flood of mud. A tender memory cracks on our temples.

Your eyes, your eyes on me, the sky splits from top to bottom, terror draws an empty canvas,

Fever roams in this desert, the earth trembles, old pulverized spine.

Your hands, your hands on my heart, a little longer still, a little longer, mad prayer,

The blood in your veins pulses with terror, changes into a monster, all fury mocked, hear this enormous laugh shake a thousand felled forests,

Your mouth on mine, dust and cinders come; love, lost love.

Hatred and war, remember, remember, wounded love, that tall cool jar spilled at your side, it was summer.

Amassed black winters growl; your strength, your strength, friend, who disarmed you, seizing your heart like a catapult?

And you and me, and me and you, and you with me! Alive! We'll crawl out of this well, death's face isn't so large that it can bar the entrance forever.

Silence grows in my mouth like an herb. One day all words were given to me. Find only this cry.

Pillaged house. Open heart. Last season. More than this cry in the pit of my stomach. Fountain of blood. Cry. Recalling you in vain, love, murdered love.

AMOUR

Toi, chair de ma chair, matin, midi, nuit, toutes mes heures et mes saisons ensemble

Toi, sang de mon sang, toutes mes fontaines, la mer et mes larmes jaillissantes

Toi, les colonnes de ma maison, mes os, l'arbre de ma vie, le mât de mes voiles et tout le voyage au plus profond de moi

Toi, nerf de mes nerfs, mes plus beaux bouquets de joie, toutes couleurs éclatées

Toi, souffle de mon souffle, vents et tempêtes, le grand air de ce monde me soulève comme une ville de toile

Toi, cœur de mes yeux, le plus large regard, la plus riche moisson de villes et d'espaces du bout de l'horizon ramenée

Toi, le goût du monde; toi, l'odeur des chemins mouillés, ciels et marées sur le sable confondus

Toi, corps de mon corps, ma terre, toutes mes forêts, l'univers chavire entre mes bras

Toi, la vigne et le fruit; toi, le vin et l'eau, toi, le pain et la table, communion et connaissance aux portes de la mort

Toi, ma vie, ma vie qui se desserre, fuit d'un pas léger sur la ligne de l'aube; toi, l'instant et mes bras dénoués

Toi, le mystère repris; toi, mon doux visage étranger, et le cœur qui se lamente dans mes veines comme une blessure.

LOVE

You, flesh of my flesh, morning, noon, night, all my hours and seasons together

You, blood of my blood, all my fountains, the sea and my flowing tears

You, the pillars of my house, my bones, tree of my life, mast of my sails and the whole voyage at the very depths of me

You, nerve of my nerves, my most beautiful bouquets of joy, all colors exploded

You, breath of my breath, winds and storms, the great air of this earth lifts me like a linen city

You, heart of my eyes, the largest gaze, the richest harvest of cities and space hauled back from the edge of the horizon

You, the taste of the world; you, the perfume of wet paths, seas and skies fused on the sand

You, body of my body, my earth, all my forests, the universe toppling mad in my arms

You, the vine and the fruit; you, the wine and the water; you, the bread and the table, communion and knowledge at the gates of death

You, my life, my life freeing itself, run away on the line of dawn with a fleeting step; you, the instant and my untied arms

You, the recaptured mystery; you, my soft, strange face, and the heart that laments in my veins like a wound.

ÉCLAIR

Le monde entier s'est allumé
Le jour brûle
Flambe
Mon amour se fonde comme l'éclair

LIGHTNING

The whole world caught on fire
Day burns
Flames
My love dissolves like lightning

LA CIGALE

Stridente
D'un seul trait
La cigale
Son cri à hauteur de mémoire
Perce le coeur

La boussole vire au midi
Le monde enfin se détraque

Du fin fond du bout du jour
L'éclat mûr du soleil
S'établit sur toutes choses

L'hiver brûle sur la place

THE CICADA

Strident
With just one note
The cicada
Its cry as high as memory
Pierces the heart

The compass turns toward noon
The world finally breaks down

From the day's utter depths
The ripe flash of the sun
Settles on everything

Winter burns in the square

EN CAS DE MALHEUR

Ferme la mer comme un lit
Tire l'eau lisse sans un pli
Iode goémon verre liquide

En cas de malheur
Que la profondeur de l'eau
Demeure
A ta portée

Songe à l'euphorie du nageur fluide
A la vitesse de son coeur
De l'autre côté du miroir
Il respire largement
Dans l'étirement de sa joie

La vie étrange luit dans ses cheveux
Comme le sel.

IF YOU'RE UNHAPPY

Close the sea like a bed
Pull back the smooth unwrinkled water
Iodine seaweed liquid glass

If you're unhappy
Let the depth of the water
Remain
Within reach

Dream of the fluid swimmer's euphoria
The speed of his heart
On the back side of the mirror
He breathes largely
In the stretch of his joy

A strange life glows in his hair
Like salt

PLUIE

Pluie sur la ville qui s'ébroue, ses cheveux de pierre aux fontaines, sabots, crinières, beaux griffons, fument les rues mouillées, roulent les quais rouillés

Toi, ta force et ton sommeil, ton rêve sous ta paupière, amande noire au cœur de la nuit, ton bras sur mes reins, comme une ceinture

Pluie sur la vitre, faufils, aiguilles liquides; de grands métiers tremblent, lissent ton sort et le mien, tisserands aveugles, rivières, fleuves, la nuit, navettes et fuseaux, se dévide, forêt de feuilles fraîches secouées

Toi, ton rire, ton œil d'oiseau, ton visage qui luit; l'amour s'étend sur moi

Pluie, au loin l'éclat jaune des platanes, fougères aux troncs noirs, places peuplées de colères brèves, fourmilières brutes où la sagesse noue et dénoue un mince fil secret

Toi et moi, île dans la ville, sous la pluie, mis au monde, mêlés ensemble comme la terre et l'eau avant le partage

Pluie sur la vitre. Si j'abandonne ton corps couché et pars en songe aussi, soulève des arches de pluie, quite la chaleur du lit, goûte le sel des eaux marines à l'horizon roulées, toute la terre accessible, pareille à un tapis

Toi, ta parole et ton silence, ta vie et ta beauté, ton amour me ramène inlassablement, tel un rosier sauvage qu'on allume dans la nuit, sous la pluie.

RAIN

Rain on the city shaking itself, its stone hair in the fountains, hoofs, manes, handsome griffins, the wet streets steaming, rusted piers rolling

You, your power and your sleep, your dream under your eyelid, black almond at the heart of night, your arm around my waist like a belt

Rain on the window pane, tacking threads, liquid needles; great looms tremble, bind your fate and mine, blind weavers, rivers, floods, the night unwinds, shuttles and spindles, a forest of fresh shaken leaves

You, your laughter, your bird's eye, your shining face; love stretches out over me

Rain, in the distance the yellow explosion of plane-trees, ferns with black trunks, places peopled with brief angers, brute ant-hills where wisdom ties and unties a thin secret thread

You and me, island in the city, in the rain, brought into the world, mingled together like earth and water before the division

Rain on the window pane. If I leave your lying body and also walk away in a dream, raise arches of rain, abandon the warmth of the bed, taste the salt of sea-water rolled to the horizon, the whole world accessible, like a carpet

You, your word and your silence, your life and your beauty, your love tirelessly brings me back, like a wild rosebush we set on fire in the night, in the rain.

NOËL

Noël, vieille rosace encrassée par les siècles, tant de patines charbonneuses aux tympans des cathédrales, masques et chimères aux fronts des hommes, miel, sucre et tilleul aux cœurs des femmes, guirlandes magiques aux mains des enfants,

Vétuste tableau noir où crisse la craie des dictées millénaires, passons l'éponge, vieil écolier, regarde le revers de ta manche, la suie du monde y laisse des lichens d'ébène,

Femme, essuie tes larmes, la promesse, depuis le point du jour, claironne la joie, que ton œil voit sans mentir ces beaux vaisseaux en rade − cargaisons amères, crève en mer le cœur gonflé de rêve,

Voix d'ange à l'oreille du berger sommeillant: «Paix aux hommes de bonne volonté», mot de passe repris en chœur par de grandes guerres, battant le ventre du monde, l'une appelant l'autre, pareilles aux marées d'équinoxe déferlant sur le sable,

Roulement de blessés, vingt siècles en marche, germent les morts aux champs, graines folles au hasard des printemps hâtifs; les visages de l'amour se perdent à mesure, clignent entre nos mains, feux minuscules, brassées de coquelicots froissés,

Ceux qu'on aime, ceux qu'on hait, tressés ensemble, doux chapelets, beaux oignons sauvages aux greniers pleins de vent; mémoires ouvertes, vastes salles tendues pour le retour d'un seul pas dans l'escalier,

Tant d'innocents entre deux gendarmes, le crime au front, gravé avec application, par un scribe, par un notaire, par un juge, par un prêtre, par toute sagesse prostituée, tout pouvoir usurpé, toute haine légalisée,

NOEL

Noel, ancient rose-window encrusted by centuries, the lustre of so much coal dust on the tympana of cathedrals, masks and chimeras on the brows of men, honey, sugar and linden in the hearts of women, magic garland in children's hands,

Decrepit blackboard where the dictations of millenia grate, use the sponge, old student, look at the back of your sleeve, the soot of the world leaves ebony lichens on it,

Woman, wipe your tears, ever since daybreak the promise has bugled joy, without lying, let your eye see those lovely moored vessels — bitter cargoes, the dream-swollen heart bursts at sea,

Angel's voice in the dozing shepherd's ear: "Peace to men of good will," pass-word picked up in chorus by great wars, battering the belly of the earth, one calling the other, like equinoctial seas unfurling on the sand,

On the march for twenty centuries, the tred of the wounded sprouts corpses in fields, mad seeds in the hazard of premature springs; the faces of love are slowly lost, blinking in our hands, minuscule fires, armfuls of bruised red poppies,

Those we love, those we hate, braided together, sweet strings of beads, lovely wild onions in windy attics; wide open memories, vast halls maintained for the return of just one footstep on the staircase,

So many innocents between two guards, the crime on the brow, diligently engraved by a scribe, by a lawyer, by a judge, by a priest, by all prostituted wisdom, all usurped power, all legalized hatred,

Qui se plaint de mourir tout seul? Quel enfant vient au monde? Quelle grand'mère, à moitié couverte par la mort, lui souffle à l'oreille que l'âme est immortelle?

Qui cherche à tâtons la face obscure de la connaissance, tandis que monte le jour, et que le cœur n'a que la tendresse des larmes pour tout recours?

Cœur. Tendresse. Larmes. Qui lave des mots dans la rivière, à grande eau; les plus perdus, les plus galvaudés, les plus traînés, les plus trahis?

Qui face à l'injustice offre son visage ruisselant, qui nomme la joie à droite et le malheur à gauche, qui recommence le matin comme une nativité?

Noël. Amour. Paix. Quel chercheur d'or, dans le courant, rince le sable et les cailloux? Pour un seul mot qui s'écale comme une noix, surgit l'éclat du Verbe à sa naissance.

Who complains of dying alone? What child is being born? What grandmother, half-covered by death, whispers in his ear that the soul is immortal?

Who gropes for the obscure face of knowledge, while day rises and the heart has but the tenderness of tears as its only recourse?

Heart. Tenderness. Tears. Who scrubs words in the wide open waters of the rivers; the most lost, the most dishonored, the most downtrodden, the most betrayed?

Who, facing injustice, offers a streaming face, who names joy on the right and agony on the left, who starts the morning afresh like a nativity?

Noel. Love. Peace. What panner for gold rinses sand and stones in the stream? For just one word shelling itself like a nut, the flash of the Word soars at its birth.

ET LE JOUR FUT

Pain, vin, fruits, amour, pays, saisis aux douanes étrangères,

Tous debout, les bras contre le corps, en flagrant délit d'attention,

Et la tendresse du jour autour de nous comme une eau bleue.

Que chacun réclame son dû, vieille échéance, âme et noyau des fureurs et du cri,

L'instant présent rayonne, douceur, fleur et pulpe, toute la terre, bel anneau calme, gravite autour du cœur justicier.

Main mise sur la ville entière, regards aux poings comme des torches,

Connaissance sur les places ouvertes, l'arbre de la parole fait de l'ombre pour tout un peuple brûlé de colère.

Qui dit son ressentiment éprouve son cœur au côté comme une arme fraîche,

Qui nomme le feu, le voit en face qui bouge tout en fleurs comme un buisson de vie,

Le jardin sera très grand, sous de hautes maîtrises d'eaux et de forêts, bien en terre, bien en souffle, et toutes feuilles lisibles dans le vent,

Qui dit vent, qui dit rivière, voit la terre qui s'agenouille,

Qui dénonce les méfaits des ancêtres et l'angoisse cultivée aux fenêtres des femmes pareille à une oseille pourpre,

AND THERE WAS LIGHT

Bread, wine, fruit, love, country seized at foreign customs,

All standing, arms at our sides, in a flagrant break of attention,

And the tenderness of day around us like blue water.

Let everyone reclaim his due, old debt, soul and stone of furies and the cry,

The present moment radiates, mildness, flower and pulp, the whole earth, lovely calm ring, revolves around the justice-loving heart.

Hand laid on the whole city, the stare of fists like torches,

Understanding in open spaces, the tree of the word is shade for a whole nation burnt by anger.

Whoever speaks his resentment, feels his heart nearby like a fresh weapon,

Whoever names the fire, sees it face to face, stirring everything into bloom like a bush of life,

The garden will be very large, under the great mastery of waters and forests, good earth, good breath, and all leaves legible in the wind,

Whoever says wind, whoever says river, sees the earth kneeling down,

Whoever denounces the wrongs of ancestors and the anguish cultivated at the window sills of women like a purple sorrel,

Retrouve la force de ses bras et l'allégeance de sa joie entre ses doigts pacifiés,

Qui prononce clairement le mot magie et lave à grande eau les pierres sacrées, délie le bouc et l'agneau, condamne la fleur du sacrifice au flanc du prêtre et des esclaves.

Tout sortilège dissipé, le bel effort dur contre la vérité dans sa terre originelle,

Notre droit devant nous à débarbouiller tel une monnaie enfouie sous la peur,

Nos paumes arrachant la malédiction comme un masque pourri,

Nos yeux, nos mains, nos lèvres se reconnaissant, l'homme et la femme inextricables sous le désir, broussaille d'épines et de lait, l'amour vendangé en plein midi,

L'enfant crie dans nos veines. Et pour sa rentrée au monde, nous lui offrirons la démarche souveraine de celle qui goûte l'aube dans ses deux mains, pour y faire boire le fils de l'homme.

Rediscovers the strength of arms and the allegiance of joy between pacified fingers,

Whoever clearly pronounces the word "magic" and washes the sacred stones in wide-open water, unbinds the buck and the ewe, condemns the sacrificial flower at the flank of the priest and the slaves.

All spells dispelled, the handsome hard effort against truth in its primeval earth,

Our right in front of us to be cleaned up like silver buried under fear,

Our palms tearing off the curse like a rotten mask,

Our eyes, our hands, our lips recognize themselves, man and woman inextricable in desire, underbrush of thorns and milk, love harvested at high noon,

The child cries in our veins. And for his entry into the world we'll offer him the sovereign procession of one who tastes dawn in her two hands so that the son of man can drink it.

TERRE ORIGINELLE

Pays reçu au plus creux du sommeil
L'arbre amer croît sur nous
Son ombre au plus haut de l'éveil
Son silence au cœur de la parole
Son nom à graver sur champ de neige.
Et toi, du point du jour ramené,
Laisse ce songe ancien aux rives du vieux monde
Pense à notre amour, l'honneur en est suffisant
L'âge brut, la face innocente et l'œil grand ouvert.
L'eau douce n'est plus de saison
La femme est salée comme l'algue
Mon âme a goût de mer et d'orange verte.
Forêts alertées rivières dénouées chantent les eaux-mères de ce
        temps
Tout un continent sous un orage de vent.
Et route, bel amour, le monde se fonde comme une ville de
        toile
S'accomplisse la farouche ressemblance du cœur
Avec sa terre originelle.

ORIGINAL EARTH

Land received in deepest sleep
The bitter tree grows above us
Its shade at the peak of awakening
Its silence at the heart of the word
Its name to be carved in a field of snow.
And you, brought back to daybreak,
Leave this ancient dream on the old world's shores
Think of our love, the honor is sufficient
Brute age, innocent face and wide-open eye.
Soft water is no longer in season
The woman is as salty as algae
My soul tastes of sea and green orange.
Alerted forests, unleashed rivers singing time's primal waters
A whole continent under a wind storm.
And starting out, handsome love, the world founds itself like a
    city of linen.
Let the heart's wild resemblance
To its original earth be accomplished.

ANNE HÉBERT:
A SELECTED BIBLIOGRAPHY

POETRY

Les Songes en équilibre. Montréal: Éditions de l'Arbre, 1942.
Le Tombeau des rois. Québec: Institut Littéraire du Québec, 1953.
Poèmes. Paris: Éditions du Seuil, 1960.
St.-Denys Garneau and Anne Hébert. Translated by Frank Scott. Vancouver: Klanak Press, 1962. (Nine poems from *Poèmes*.)
The Tomb of Kings. Translated by Peter Miller. Toronto: Contact Press, 1967.
[Thirteen Poems.] Translated by F. R. Scott, G. V. Downes and Ralph Gustafson. In *The Poetry of French Canada in Translation*. Edited by John Glassco. Toronto: Oxford University Press, 1970.
Poems by Anne Hébert. Translated by Alan Brown. Don Mills, Ontario: Musson Books, 1975.
[Seven Poems.] Translated by Fred Cogswell. In *Poetry of Modern Québec*. Edited by Fred Cogswell. Montréal: Harvest House, 1976.
Poems. Translated by A. Poulin, Jr.. In *Quarterly Review of Literature XXI*: Nos. 3/4, Poetry Series, 1980. (Thirty-two poems from *Poèmes*.)
[Nine Poems.] Translated by Aliki Barnstone, Willis Barnstone, Maxine Kumin and A. Poulin, Jr.. In *A Book of Women Poets from Antiquity to Now*. Edited by Aliki Barnstone and Willis Barnstone. New York: Shocken Books, 1980.

FICTION

Le Torrent. Montréal: Éditions Beauchemin, 1950; 2nd enlarged edition, Montréal: Éditions HMH, 1963; European edition, Paris: Éditions du Seuil, 1965.

Les Chambres de bois. Paris: Éditions du Seuil, 1958.

Kamouraska. Paris: Éditions du Seuil, 1970.

The Torrent: Novellas and Short Stories. Translated by Gwendolyn Moore. Montréal: Harvest House, 1973.

Kamouraska. Translated by Norman Shapiro. Don Mills, Ontario: Musson Books, 1972; New York: Crown Publishers, 1973; Don Mills, Ontario: General Publishing Paperbacks, 1982.

The Silent Rooms. Translated by Kathy Mezei. Don Mills, Ontario: Musson Books, 1974.

Les Enfants du Sabbat. Paris: Éditions du Seuil, 1975.

Children of the Black Sabbath. Translated by Carol Dunlop-Hébert. Don Mills, Ontario: Musson Books, 1977; New York: Crown Publishers, 1977; Don Mills, Ontario: General Publishing Paperbacks, 1982.

Héloïse. Paris: Éditions du Seuil, 1980.

Les Fous de bassan. Paris: Éditions du Seuil, 1982.

Héloïse. Translated by Sheila Fischman. Don Mills, Ontario: Stoddart Publishing Co., Ltd., 1982; Don Mills, Ontario: General Publishing Paperbacks, 1984; New York: Beaufort Publishing, Inc., 1984.

In the Shadow of the Wind. Translated by Sheila Fischman. Don Mills, Ontario: Stoddart Publishing Co., Ltd., 1983; Don Mills, Ontario: General Publishing Paperbacks, 1984; New York: Beaufort Publishing Inc., 1984.

DRAMA

Le Temps sauvage. Montréal: Éditions HMH, 1967.

OTHER

Dialogue sur la traduction: à propos du "Tombeau des rois." Anne Hébert et Frank Scott. Présentation de Jeanne Lapointe; Préface de Northrop Frye. Montréal: Éditions HMH, 1970.

POETRY AND THE LANDSCAPE OF EPIPHANY: ON TRANSLATING THE POETRY OF ANNE HÉBERT

My interest in Anne Hébert's poetry—as well as in the work of other Québecois poets—is rooted in considerations that are as much personal and political as they are literary. But then all art is as much an epiphany of encounter with one's total personality as it is a tongue shaping the confrontation with one's medium at the heart of silence.

I was born in a small inland town in New England into a family of French-Canadians—also known as Franco-Americans, Canucks, Frogs and, with somewhat more recent ethnic diplomacy, Québecois-Americans. My mother's parents seem to have emigrated to the United States and to Lisbon, Maine, without much fanfare some time before she was born; ironically, their somewhat demure arrival into the United States may have been due to the fact that her paternal grandmother was reputedly Irish (thus probably risking being Protestant, too). My father's utterly Catholic parents packed their nine kids into a rented car and headed south in a more tribal fashion when he was still a child. In either case, ours was and—even twenty some-odd years after most of us have moved away from Lisbon and though our numbers now include corporate vice-presidents and college professors—at wakes, weddings and anniversaries of one kind or another, ours still continues to be a thoroughly French-Canadian family whose essential characteristics are seeded deeply amidst the roots of our communal sensuous life.

An American by birth, I first spoke French—actually a hodgepodge *patois* of medieval French, French-Canadian "joual" (i.e. "horse language") and a fractured Frank-glish—before I began speaking a heavily French-accented Downeast Yankee English taught to me primarily by Verna Dingley, my Yankee childhood friend's mother so that her son and I could play together. Despite gestures toward assimilation by my parents (school clothes that were always just a little too new and just a little too neat), most of my childhood was seeped in the mores of my French-Canadian ancestors and in their "manners," what Lionel Trilling described as "the hum and buzz of implication . . . that part of a culture which is made up of half-uttered or unuttered or unutterable expressions of value."

And in their overt customs, too: a primary education at St. Bernadette's, the parochial school run by the good sisters of the Presentation of Mary in St. Anne's Parish, where the curriculum included Catechism classes every day and *l'Histoire Sainte* (a mixture of hagiography and Church history taught in French, the language of our Roman Catholic faith, and inculcating in us the conviction that St. Laurence's martyrdom consisted of being barbecued to death); Father Leo J. Bourque celebrating Holy Mass at seven o'clock every morning of the year, the good sisters in the sacristy an hour ahead of time to lay out the vestments, fill the cruets with water and wine and prepare the altar; (in feverish glare I still see Sister Mary Edmond's and Sister Jean-Marie's black habits billowing in swirling clouds of ice-gray snow in March as they walk silently to Church in semi-darkness); Father Bourque coming to our classes once a month to read our report cards in public, praising the successful and reprimanding the sluggards; a closely knit family of tribal life involving literally dozens of aunts, uncles and cousins that rivaled any Gilbert and Sullivan operetta and often clustered around religious observances, holidays, family crises, and always returning to memory with the odors of wine, pure beeswax, incense, pork pies, baked beans and whiskey on the lips of the grown-ups.

From birth to death our lives were governed by grand and sacred concentric calendars ruling virtually all measures of time, from the seemingly endless seasons to individual and all too breathless hours of worship or play. And during some of those hours Harold Dingley made fun of my Canuck accent, teased me because I had to go to Mass every morning during Lent, or tried to get me to eat hot-dogs on Fridays. A few days before my First Communion, Harold threw a rock at me. A small sliver of that childhood stone is still lodged in my forehead and unleashes a sharp pain when I press it.

My aunts steamed their kitchens with preserves and pickles, with the bleach of their Monday-morning wash. My uncles' clothes reeked with the oil of wool and cotton mills where they worked; at night they sat on their front porches and drank warm beers late into the darkness, the stars of their cigarettes burning silently, ferociously in the gravel of their lungs. And they died — leaving clinging presences:

CASTLE LIFE

This is the family castle
Without a fire or table,
Without carpets or dust.

The perverse enchantment of this place
Is looking into mirrors day and night.

Throw your reflection into those hard pools,
Your hardest one without shadow or color.

See, those mirrors are deep
As chests.
Some ghost is always there behind the lead
And quickly covers your reflection,
Clings to you like algae,

Adjusts itself to you, thin and naked,
Counterfeiting love in a slow bitter shiver.

Most French-Canadian-Americans or Franco-American-Canucks of my generation . . . and that's exactly what we were and were not: neither French, nor Canadian, nor genuinely American—we spent the better part of our adolescence and early childhood working feverishly hard at negating and trying to erase all traces of our Québecois heritage. First the accent, then the language, then the faith, the customs, the manners—anything that could be scraped, shaved or singed off.

Long before the phrase became popular in the Province of Québec at the start of the Separatist Movement, we had come to know and feel viscerally that we were the "White Niggers" of New England. And we were hell-bent on becoming categorically assimilated (this time Calvin Klein and Bill Blass), on "making it" in any man's world other than the fiber factories of our French-Canadian fathers in Lewiston, Maine, in any woman's world other than the kitchens of our Franco-American mothers in Lowell, Massachusetts, where, even as in Québec, in the words of Anne Hébert, "the man smells the bread burning, and the center of the day collapses on us like water without seams."

And yet, after private school in Hyde Park, New York, college in Chicago, and the University in Iowa, after the start of a professional career, ostensibly assimilated by a WASP society as much as possible, some of us eventually realized that we also had severed ourselves from a vital source of our total selves, that source where the blood that feeds the soul is brewed. Having renounced the hum and buzz of a culture's implication, we also had precluded the possibility of any fruitful encounter with the living heart of the culture itself.

If we knew something about the culture of Germany and Japan, we knew nothing about our ancestral culture that eventually would play a central role in a people's evolution from the ennui of being nothing better than French-Canadian to a growing zealous pride in being Québecois. If we knew all we were expected to know about the literatures of England and America in order to pass Ph.D. comprehensive exams to become professors, we were ignorant of the voices and of the literature of our tribal sisters and brothers. (Indeed, some of us had been professors for years before realizing or at least admitting that even Jack Kerouac had been one of us all along–and he'd helped to radicalize our entire generation.) In short, we realized that in the very process of assimilation (even in our Pierre Cardins and Yves St. Laurents) we simply had become transformed from factory-working to cultural and spiritual "White Niggers."

Not until 1962-63, when I returned to Maine to teach at St. Francis College, did I have any idea that there was such a thing as "French-Canadian" or "Québecois" poetry. Not until one of my young French-Canadian colleagues from Ottawa, Michel Gaulin, loaned me a copy of *Poèmes* had I even heard of Anne Hébert who, even in the early 60's, was already widely recognized throughout the French-speaking world as modern Québec's greatest poet and one of the great *French* poets in the world.

My interest in Anne Hébert's poetry, then, is quite personal: the world of these poems is the physical and emotional landscape where a vital part of my personality as a person and as an artist is rooted, that part I'm attempting to graft back onto my total self. As Hébert has written in "Poetry: Loneliness Broken," this landscape is of a country perhaps no older "than the earth's first days. Life here has to be discovered and be named; our obscure face, our silent heart, these pre-human landscapes waiting to be inhabited and ruled by us, and this confused tongue of ours that murmurs in the dark–all that calls for day and light."

My interest in Anne Hébert's poetry turns out to be political, too, in so far as the poems themselves are political in the most profound sense of that word. No less than the work of her contemporaries around the world, Hébert also speaks of a national "anguish and isolation" that is as much a political reality as it is a psychological and/or emotional presence in one's personal, ethnic history.

Moreover, surely one can't read Anne Hébert's poems (most of them written before 1960) without realizing that she was committed to the essential and profound principles of feminism–liberating men as much as it liberates women–long before it was fashionable to be so (although she adamantly insists that she is not a "feminist.") Moreover, the final thrust of her poems clearly reflects Hébert's agreement with Camus (slightly adapted): "If she speaks or reasons, especially if she writes, immediately our sister extends her hand, the tree is justified, love is born. A literature of despair is a contradiction in terms."

But my interest in Anne Hébert's work is also genuinely literary and professional. As I stated earlier, she is generally recognized throughout the French-speaking world (and not only in Canada) as one of the great French poets whose work has been translated into several languages. She is also generally recognized as French Canada's greatest living novelist, whose books include *Kamouraska* (1970), *Les Enfants du sabbat* (1975), *Héloïse* (1980) and *Les Fous de bassan* (1982). She has been the recipient of virtually every major literary award in Canada, including the Prix France-Canada (1958), Prix de la Province du Québec (1959), Prix du Gouveneur Général (for poetry, 1961; for fiction, 1975), Prix Molson du Conseil des Arts au Canada (1967) and the prestigeous Prix David from the Province of Québec for the whole of her work (1978). Moreover, she has been the recipient of several major awards in France, including the Prix des Libraries (1971), the Grand Prix du Roman from l'Académie française (1976) and Le Prix Fémina (1982). In 1982 she was also nominated for the Prix Goncourt in France for her novel *Les Fous de bassson*. Meanwhile, there is no doubt in the minds of many that Anne Hébert is a natural candidate for an eventual Nobel Prize for Literature.

In light of her international reputation as a poet and as a novelist, it's rather ironic that most readers of poetry–and indeed, many poets–in the United States have never heard of Anne Hébert. In large part that is due to a certain measure of cultural imperialism in the U.S. academic/literary community which, out of lingering ignorance and prejudice, relegates the work of most Québecois poets and novelists to some exotic category of "folk literature" written in a strange dialect, i.e., "joual," i.e., "horse talk." And yet few French Houyhnhnms have been nominated for the Prix Goncourt or considered for the Nobel Prize. While the literary community in the United States knows a great deal about South American, European and Asian literature in translation, we know virtually nothing at all about the French literature written by our brothers and sisters who inhabit this North American continent with us.

Along with Saint-Denys Garneau, Rina Lasnier, and Alain Grandbois—whose first important books of poetry all appeared in the early 1940's—Anne Hébert is generally recognized as one of the founders of modern/contemporary poetry in Québec. The full reasons for the importance of those poets' role in the evolution of French poetry in Canada since World War II are too complex even to be sketched in broad strokes in a brief statement such as this one. However, it is important to say that, whether consciously pursued or not, the work of those four poets was at least an implicit bid to establish a poetry that was not the provincial voice of a European French culture, but rather an aesthetically viable poetry rooted in and giving voice to a thoroughly New World, North American, Québecois experience and sensibility in a uniquely intimate and cultured language and music. It was also an equally strong bid to write a purely secular poetry that was neither in the service of Roman Catholicism nor immersed in and projecting the piety of a Roman sensibility.

Anne Hébert's first book of poems, *Les Songes en équilibre*, appeared in 1942, when the poet was only 26. The title of that book—*The Counterbalanced Dreams*— was indicative of its youthful contents and style. With their impressionistic and incantatory lines of only three or four syllable-breaths, the poems dealt largely with a nostalgia for childhood, as well as with a youthful sense of sorrow and solitude, the mystery of a crystal-like (and clearly inexperienced) love. As one critic has noted, *Les Songes en équilibre* was a kind of "plaintif elegy" for an image of childhood that was at least protected, if it wasn't entirely happy, and of a life in an environment that was at least favorable to "childish joys," if it wasn't genuinely exciting. In short, the poems were somewhat breathless lyrics in which the young Hébert seemingly attempted to counterbalance the experience of reality with the experience of a more private, "poetic" and perhaps gratuitous dream-world. (Hébert herself now considers the poems in *Les Songes en équilibre* as juvenalia and refuses to allow them to be reprinted or translated.)

Between the publication of *Les Songes en équilibre* and the appearance of her second book, *Le Tombeau des rois* (*The Tomb of Kings*) in 1953, Anne Hébert underwent a profound aesthetic maturity which, some critics speculate, may have been rooted in a complex of equally profound personal experiences. (Critics are also quick to suggest that the premature and mysterious death of her cousin, friend and mentor, Saint-Denys Garneau, after a long and troubled period of isolation and ostensible silence, must have been an important factor.)

The factual reasons for Hébert's artistic transformation are probably irrelevant. What is important is that she seems to have undergone some kind of personal and aesthetic dark night of the soul out of which emerged the more fiercely personal and darker vision of the poems in *Le Tombeau des rois*. Subsequently, that vision, intensity, and power assumed greater metaphysical and oracular dimensions that informed the poems in *Mystère de la parole* (*The Mystery of the Word*) which, together with those in *The Tomb of Kings*, were issued as *Poèmes* (Paris, 1960) – the book that confirmed Anne Hébert's reputation as one of French-Canada's and of the French-speaking world's great poets.

The mature poems of Anne Hébert are indeed fiercely personal. Without resorting to the personal-confessional mode of her American contemporaries, Hébert's poems, especially in *The Tomb of Kings*, trace the contours of a woman's private and intense emotional life within a recognizable middle-class landscape. Hébert's vision of both the self and the non-self is clearly not a cause for cautious celebration or for lyricism; rather, those later poems project a vision of increasing isolation, dislocation, deterioration, horror and despair. Moreover, because of a certain seeming timidity of public gesture, as well as the intimate correlatives and symbology controlling emotion and experience, those poems also almost risk being hermetic.

The personal vision in *The Tomb of Kings* intensifies even more in *The Mystery of the Word*, as well as in her uncollected poems generally written between 1964 and 1969, and becomes the foundation on which Anne Hébert erects another kind of personal poetry of metaphysical and oracular proportions, a personal history fired to the pitch of visionary ethics—a vision that penetrates to the heart of experience, to the heart of silence, where the poet's hard passion re-invents the image of an inhabitable human place (especially for herself and her sisters) and invokes the primal earth-mother, Eve, to "rediscover the shade of grace on [her] face like a black beam." Reading these poems by Anne Hébert, one is reminded of the concluding lines of Adrienne Rich's poem, "Planetarium," in which the American poet asserts:

> I am an instrument in the shape
> of a woman trying to translate pulsations
> into images for the relief of the body
> and the reconstruction of the mind

Anne Hébert's epiphany is no less a healing song:

> Let the heart's wild resemblance
> To its original earth be accomplished.

ABOUT THE AUTHOR

Born in Sainte-Catherine-de-Fossambault, Québec, in 1916, Anne Hébert is internationally reknowned as a major world poet and Canada's most important French poet of the 20th century. Her novels—*Kamouraska, Les Enfants du sabbat, Héloïse* and *Les Fous de bassan*—are also recognized as masterpieces of contemporary French fiction. She has been the recipient of every major literary award in Canada, including the Prix du Gouverneur Général, the Prix David de la Province du Québec, the Prix France-Canada and the Prix Molson du Conseil des Arts au Canada, and several major awards in France, including the Prix des Librairies, the Grand Prix du Roman de l'Académie française and the Prix Femina, as well as being nominated for the Prix Goncourt. Since 1955 she has divided her time between Canada and France. *Anne Hébert: Selected Poems* is the first bilingual collection of her poetry published in the United States.

ABOUT THE TRANSLATOR

A. Poulin, Jr. was born in Lisbon, Maine, in 1938 of French-Canadian immigrant parents. The recipient of grants for both poetry and translation from the National Endowment for the Arts, the Translation Center of Columbia University, (for translation), The New York Foundation for the Arts (for poetry) and a Faculty Programme Enrichment grant from the Embassy of Canada, Mr. Poulin's most recent book of poems is *A Momentary Order* (Graywolf Press, 1987). He is also the highly acclaimed translator of *The Complete French Poems of Rainer Maria Rilke* (Graywolf Press, 1986) and Rilke's *Duino Elegies and The Sonnets to Orpheus* (Houghton Mifflin, Co., 1977). A Professor of English at the State University of New York, College at Brockport, and Founding Editor-Publisher of BOA Editions, Ltd., he currently resides in Brockport, New York, with the jeweler and metalsmith, Basilike Poulin, and their daughter, Daphne.

BOA EDITIONS, LTD.
NEW AMERICAN TRANSLATION SERIES